Making a
Difference
in
Preaching

Also by Scott M. Gibson
The Big Idea of Biblical Preaching: Connecting the Bible to People

Also by Haddon Robinson
Biblical Preaching
Biblical Sermons
Christian Salt and Light Company
Decision Making by the Book
Grief
What Jesus Said about Christian Living

Making a Difference in Preaching

Haddon Robinson on Biblical Preaching

Scott M. Gibson, editor

Baker Books

A Division of Baker Book House Co
Grand Rapids, Michigan 49516

For Haddon W. Robinson
Preacher, colleague, mentor, and friend

Published by Baker Books
a division of Baker Book House Company
P.O. Box 6287, Grand Rapids, MI 49516-6287

Printed in the United States of America

Library of Congress Cataloging-in-Publication Data

Robinson, Haddon W.
　　Making a difference in preaching : Haddon Robinson on biblical preaching / Scott M. Gibson, editor.
　　　　p.　　cm.
　　Includes bibliographical references.
　　ISBN 0-8010-9092-X
　　1. Preaching. 2. Bible—Homiletical use. I. Gibson, Scott M., 1957–　.
II. Title.
BV4211.2.R595　1999
251—dc21　　　　　　　　　　　　　　　　　　　　　99-37518

For information about academic books, resources for Christian leaders, and all new releases available from Baker Book House, visit our web site:
http://www.bakerbooks.com

Contents

Acknowledgments

Thanks to my able secretary, Dianne Newhall, and to my student assistants, Sui-Yin Vivian Cheung, Stephen M. Lane, and Glen L. Massey for their technical support.

I am grateful to the following publishers for their permission to reproduce copyrighted material:

Thanks to *Leadership Journal* for the following: "Busting out of Sermon Block," *Leadership* 14:4 (Fall 1993): 94–99. Reprinted by permission.

"Listening to the Listeners," *Leadership* 4:2 (Spring 1983): 68–71. Reprinted by permission.

"Preaching to Everyone in Particular," *Leadership* 15:4 (Fall 1994): 99–103. Reprinted by permission.

"Preaching Sense about Dollars," *Leadership* 10:4 (Fall 1989): 90–96. Reprinted by permission.

"Preaching With a Limp," *Leadership* 15:1 (Winter 1994): 50–55. Reprinted by permission.

"What Authority Do We Have Anymore?" *Leadership* 13:2 (Spring 1992): 24–29. Reprinted by permission.

Thanks to Christianity Today, Inc., and Haddon W. Robinson for the following, "Profile of the American Clergyman," *Christianity Today* 24:10 (May 23, 1980): 631–633. Reprinted by permission.

"Competing with the Communication Kings," in *A Voice in the Wilderness: Clear Preaching in a Complicated World.* Eds., Steve Brown, Haddon Robinson, William Willimon (Sisters, OR: Multnomah, 1993) 25–33. Copyright Christianity Today, Inc. Reprinted by permission.

"Blending Biblical Content and Life Application," in *Mastering Contemporary Preaching.* Eds., Bill Hybels, Stuart Briscoe, Haddon Robinson (Sisters, OR: Multnomah, 1989) 55–65. Copyright Christianity Today, Inc. Reprinted by permission.

Thanks to the Christian Medical & Dental Society, "Testimony of a Checkbook," *Christian Medical Society Journal* 7:4 (Fall 1976): 2–5. Reprinted by permission of the Christian Medical & Dental Society, a professional membership organization of Christian doctors and students, P.O. Box 7500, Bristol, TN 37621; Ph: 423–844–1000; Web: www. cmds.org.

Thanks to The Evangelical Theological Society, "The Theologian and the Evangelist," *Journal of the Evangelical Theological Society* 28:1 (March 1985): 3–8. Reprinted by permission. Subscriptions for the *Journal of the Evangelical Theological Society* may be obtained by writing to: 112 Russell Woods Drive, Lynchburg, VA 24502–3530.

Thanks to Dallas Theological Seminary and editor of its journal, *Bibliotheca Sacra* for permission to reprint "What is Expository Preaching?" *Bibliotheca Sacra* 131:521 (January–March 1974): 55–60. Reprinted by permission.

Thanks to Zondervan Publishing House for "Homiletics & Hermeneutics," taken from *Hermeneutics, Inerrancy, & the Bible.* Eds., Earl D. Radmacher and Robert D. Preus. Copyright 1984 by The Zondervan Corporation. Used by permission of Zondervan Publishing House.

Many thanks to Keith Willhite of Dallas Theological Seminary for his willingness to write the Foreword for this book. I am grateful to Paul E. Engle of Baker Book House for his interest in this project and for his many kindnesses.

Finally, I thank Haddon W. Robinson for his permission to reprint the materials in this book. Thank you, Haddon, for your immense contribution to the field of homiletics. And thank you for your impact on my life.

Foreword

Making a Difference in Preaching gives Haddon Robinson the privilege of casting an even longer shadow than that already cast by his forty-plus years of preaching and teaching homiletics.[1] Haddon Robinson himself is a preacher of difference. Anyone who has had the joy of listening to him preach has listened to interpretive insights, masterful images, and similes and illustrations that sharpen the point or the big idea with amazing precision.

Years ago, a seminary classmate remarked, "I think God made Haddon Robinson and then he made all the rest of us—two runs of production." I responded, "I think he made Haddon Robinson, then a bunch of other preachers, and then the rest of us. We were two runs removed." My classmate agreed.

I welcome *Making a Difference in Preaching* for at least three reasons: utility, history, and promise.

Utility. Rather than poking through dusty shelves in a library's periodical room, this volume unites under one cover the intuitive and scholarly perceptions of Haddon Robinson, collected from a life devoted to biblical preaching. Convenience, however, is not the only result of utility. Now, the reader can compare and contrast Robinson's perspective of the preacher as theologian, the preacher as evangelist, and the blend of biblical content and life application in a single context.

History. Robinson's paradigm for preaching grows from what the Puritans called "plain preaching": careful exegesis, identification of a theological principle, and an exact statement of a homiletical proposition or "big idea" as Robinson called it.[2] Not intentionally "Puritan," however, Robinson's approach to preaching also arises from the rhetorical theory of the clergy-rhetoricians Campbell and Whately. The roots of his developmental questions reside in Richard Whately's understanding of rhetoric as "inquiry after propositions."[3]

Promise. Students of preaching surely will profit from Robinson's colorful perspectives such as preaching with a limp (chapter 4) or the exegesis of changing a tire (chapter 7). At the dawn of a new century few can march into the next era by maintaining the marriage of biblical accuracy and communicative relevance like Haddon Robinson. Thus, the book looks forward with promise for those who will preach until Jesus returns. Sermons will continue to rise to new heights. Why? Because the preacher has read *Making a Difference in Preaching.*

We owe Scott M. Gibson our gratitude for editing this collection. Robinson's longer shadow is comforting shade in the hot light of the pulpit.

Keith Willhite
Director of Doctor of Ministry Studies
Associate Professor of Pastoral Ministries
Dallas Theological Seminary

Introduction

As a teenager Haddon W. Robinson wrote the following in his diary about the preacher Harry Ironside, "He preached for an hour and it seemed like twenty-minutes; others preach for twenty-minutes and it seems like an hour. I wonder what the difference is?" Haddon Robinson has spent the rest of his life trying to answer this question.

Haddon William Robinson was born on March 21, 1931, to William Andrew and Anna Robinson, immigrants from Ireland. They made their home in the Mousetown district of Harlem, described by *Reader's Digest* as one of the most dangerous areas in the United States.

Haddon's mother died when he was ten. He became what we now refer to as a "latch-key kid," raised by his father. His father was a dedicated Christian who worked during the afternoons and evenings. He undoubtedly prayed for his son. The rough neighborhood in which the Robinsons lived had its influence on the young boy. He associated with a gang. One night his gang was gathered for a rumble. Somehow, the police were tipped off and arrived on the scene.

A policeman approached the group in which Robinson was a member. He searched the boy and found that he had an ice pick tucked away in his clothing. "What do you plan to do with this?" barked the officer. "Chop ice," said Robinson. The officer pushed him and sent him sprawling. That night changed the young Robinson's outlook on gang membership, and answered his father's prayers.

During this time he came into contact with John Mygatt, a Sunday School teacher at the Broadway Presbyterian Church. Mygatt made the lessons exciting.

John Mygatt loved his class of boys. He was one of the few people from the church who came to the Robinson home to visit. The Sunday School teacher made a lifelong impression on the boy from Mousetown.

Sometime during his early teens Robinson prayed the sinner's prayer and gave his life to Christ. Then, at age 16 he left for college at Bob Jones University. While in college he became interested in preaching, spending Friday evenings in the library reading books of sermons and related works on the subject. During this time his interest in preaching and his skill at practicing it grew. When he graduated he received the top award given to a senior for preaching. He gave a sermon on John 3:16.

In 1951, following college, he became a postgraduate student at Dallas Theological Seminary and married his college sweetheart, Bonnie Vick.

During his final year at Dallas Seminary he taught informal classes in preaching. He left Dallas in 1955 for the First Baptist Church of Medford, Oregon, where he was assistant pastor. Robinson planned to be an evangelist, and after only a few years in Oregon, Dallas Seminary asked that he come back to teach preaching at the school. He spent 19 years at Dallas.

Robinson completed a master of arts degree at Southern Methodist University in 1960 and his doctor of philosophy in speech communication at the University of Illinois in 1964.

In 1979, Robinson became president of Denver Theological Seminary, and published his textbook on preaching, *Biblical Preaching: The Development and Delivery of Expository Messages* in 1980.

After twelve years at Denver Seminary, Robinson was invited by Gordon-Conwell Theological Seminary in Hamilton, Massachusetts, to become the Harold John Ockenga Distinguished

Professor of Preaching. He assumed the position in the fall of 1991.

Haddon Robinson has been teaching preaching for over forty years. This book is a collection of his writing on this important task. It is an attempt to answer the question he raised as a young person, "I wonder what the difference is?"

Making the Difference

For decades Haddon Robinson has been teaching preachers the difference between preaching well and preaching poorly. His discoveries are compiled in this book, a collection of articles and chapters from various sources written by Haddon Robinson on what he considers to be the elements that contribute to excellent preaching.

The book is divided into three sections. The first section, "The Preacher," has four chapters that begins with, "The Theologian and the Evangelist." The chapter is Haddon Robinson's 1984 presidential address given to the Evangelical Theological Society.

In chapter two, "What Authority Do We Have Anymore?" Robinson calls the preacher to be aware of the way in which he or she is perceived by modern men and women and why anyone should pay attention to what preachers have to say. The third chapter is "A Profile of the American Clergyman." Here, Robinson surveys the trends of American clergy as found in a *Christianity Today*–Gallup Poll. He found that in impressive numbers American clergy get involved in a personal way with needy men and women.

The final article in the section is chapter four, "Preaching With a Limp." This is a chapter about pastors and pain—the kinds of pain a pastor experiences while still having to preach, teach, and serve. One's family may be in turmoil, one's health declining, loneliness may be creeping in, or depression has become a friend—all of these may wound the preacher and intersect with one's ministry. Robinson deals with the struggles of preaching with a limp.

"The Preacher and Preaching" makes up the second section of the book. This section is devoted to Haddon Robinson's biblical and theological assumptions at the root of his central idea—Big Idea—philosophy. The first chapter in this section, chapter five, "What Is Expository Preaching?" is Haddon Robinson's defense and definition of expository preaching and is foundational for understanding his definition of preaching.

One of the biggest challenges for the preacher is hermeneutics. Chapter six, "Homiletics and Hermeneutics," is a paper Haddon Robinson submitted to the International Council on Biblical Inerrancy in which he argues that the work of exegesis, hermeneutics, and homiletics are linked together as supporting disciplines. He builds upon his definition of preaching and examines the concern for the integrity of the text and its implications for preaching.

Whereas the previous chapter established the theology of hermeneutics, chapter seven, "Blending Bible Content and Life Application," fleshes out the victories and pitfalls of application.

All preachers know that preaching is hard work. Robinson explores the preaching process, providing the preacher with helpful hints on how to move from text to sermon in chapter eight, "Busting Out of Sermon Block."

The third section, "The Preacher and People," consists of chapters urging the preacher to think intentionally about the people to whom he or she preaches. This section begins with chapter nine, "Competing with the Communication Kings." Every Sunday preachers are compared with television preachers, evangelists, mega-church pastors—communication kings. Robinson tackles the issue by admitting the virtues of the kings, but also recognizing the advantages a local pastor has with his or her congregation.

In chapter ten, "Preaching to Everyone in Particular," Haddon Robinson wants preachers to recognize that understanding one's audience is key to preaching. He urges preachers to speak to a cross section in the church and to target particular audiences.

In "Listening to the Listeners," chapter eleven, Robinson reminds us that feedback is the lifeblood of communication. With it, preaching touches life. Connecting with one's listeners is another key to good preaching and Robinson provides tips to do just that.

Two chapters are given to preaching about money, "Preaching Sense about Dollars" and "Testimony of a Checkbook." In chapter twelve, Robinson acknowledges that preaching about money can be difficult. It's a connection with one's listeners that can make the preacher (and congregation) uneasy. Haddon Robinson deals with the sensitive issue of preaching about money and the Christian's responsibility—as well as the preacher's responsibility to preach about it.

For a number of years Robinson was the director of the Christian Medical Society. The second chapter on money, chapter thirteen, was written for the Society's journal and deals with the particular issue of giving, and how Christians are called to be responsible givers.

The thoughtful reader will find that Haddon Robinson has answered the question he raised as a teenager: "I wonder what the difference is?" His teaching, preaching, and writing on preaching have helped scores of preachers to make a difference in their own preaching.

The Preacher

The Theologian and the Evangelist

In 1966 a World Congress on Evangelism was held in Berlin, West Germany. While the honorary chairman of that gathering was evangelist Billy Graham, the acting chairman was Carl F. H. Henry, the noted American theologian and editor of *Christianity Today*.

At the opening session of the Congress, Henry introduced Graham to the delegates by saying something like this: "Several years ago, after Billy Graham graduated from Wheaton College, I urged him to go on to seminary. Fortunately, Billy did not take my advice. Had he done so, we might have lost the most effective evangelist of our generation."

While Henry, the distinguished scholar, made that comment with a touch of jest, educators sitting in the audience shifted uneasily in their seats. Theological education and evangelism have too often made an oil-and-water mix. A survey of the noted evangelists of the last two centuries reveals that few had a seminary education. Scores of earnest Christians suspect that seminary graduates have "emptied the churches by degrees," and the slip of the tongue that turns "seminary" into "cemetery" has strong Freudian overtones.

Yet this antagonism between theology and evangelism developed in recent history. Theological scholarship came under suspicion when it was infected by German criticism. During the last two hundred years the most savage attacks made on the historic Christian faith have come from professing Christians. German critics starting with Bruno Baur, fortified by the agnostic philosophy of Immanuel Kant and the idealism of Hegel, produced rationalism. These scholars wrote off evangelical Christianity as outmoded and out of step with the times. They devoted their brilliant intellects and sharpened pens to ripping apart the pages of Scripture. They took the miracles out of history, the fire out of hell, and the deity out of Jesus, and they left the Bible in shreds. The Old Testament was dismissed as fables about a tribal god, and the New Testament documents were treated like old letters from a distant time stored in the attic of religion.

German criticism arose at the same time that changes took place in American theological education. Before the Revolutionary War, young men prepared for the ministry by living in the homes of older ministers. The younger and older men would study the Bible together, read theology, and discuss church history, and then they would move about the parish visiting the sick and instructing families.

While this initial approach to theological education had the obvious advantage of keeping the theoretical and practical together, it had serious problems. Not all the older ministers could provide the breadth of training the younger pastors needed. Gradually, church leaders felt the need for more consistent education for the clergy, and they turned to the colleges to provide it. Seminaries emerged first as graduate schools of religion, and those who taught in them were selected because of their education. Professors in the schools were enamored with the latest scholarship that came from the Continent, and the critical views taught in the classroom filtered down through the students to the churches.

Unfortunately, seminaries were seldom held accountable to local congregations. The schools received handsome endowments from wealthy individuals or denominations and, as a result, scholars in the schools did not pay much attention to what their teaching did to the churches. If men and women in the pews felt they were drinking from a muddy stream, they were powerless to clean up the spiritual pollution.

Seminaries and Evangelism

Theologians in the seminaries often belittled evangelism. Evangelists were dismissed as unscholarly and noisy nuisances. Many in the churches, on the other side, reacted against seminaries and scholarship. In their eyes, theology appeared as both unnecessary and dangerous. Revivals under evangelists like Charles Finney, D. L. Moody, Sam Jones, Bob Jones, and Billy Sunday—all theologically uneducated—brought into the church converts who saw little need for ministers with seminary training. For them evangelism stood as the only need of the hour, and at the turn of the twentieth century, Bible institutes were founded that minimized theology and put their emphasis on practical training. The rise of faith missions heightened the place of evangelism. Without doubt the Bible institutes and faith missions provided a needed correction within the church, but often at the price of theological reflection.

What is more, members of the scholarly community had reason to suspect evangelists. Some were little more than irresponsible sensationalists more concerned with nickels and numbers than people. When Sinclair Lewis wrote *Elmer Gantry*, he pointed to a disgraceful condition in which some evangelists manipulated their congregations and, in the name of God, fleeced them instead of feeding them. Throughout large sections of the country, people looked forward to the circus and the revival as the major community events of the year. In fact, the two had much in common. Both were held in tents, both attracted the entire community, and at times the only observable difference was that at the circus you paid for the entertainment before you entered the tent, while at the revival your money was collected on the inside. Many evangelists entered the ministry with little more than a sensational life story and ten sermons, and they kept on the move to preach them to different crowds. Education was suspect. "If a little knowledge is a dangerous thing," they reasoned, "how much more dangerous would a lot of learning be!"

The separation of theology and evangelism proved a tragic divorce. The evangelist and the theologian are both needed today. Evangelism without sound doctrine decays into ignorant fanaticism. Theology without the goal of making converts degenerates into cold intellectualism. The result of this separation is a faith that is neither intellectually nor biblically sound nor spiritually satisfying. The people of God need to appreciate both the theologian and the evangelist.

The Theologian and the Evangelist

We can observe both callings at work in two outstanding leaders of the church in the eighteenth century. John Wesley was an evangelist. He was born into a home where, in his growing-up years, religion shaped his life. Yet it was as an adult that he was converted to Christ. After studying for the ministry at Oxford, Wesley traveled to the United States as a missionary to the American Indians. Discouraged with his efforts, he returned home to England. One evening Wesley was invited to attend a religious meeting at Aldersgate, where he listened to the reading of Martin Luther's preface to the book of Romans. In those moments Wesley felt his heart "strangely warmed" and through that experience became truly converted.

John Wesley plunged into an exhausting evangelistic ministry. Preaching two to five sermons a day, he preached at least 40,000 sermons in his lifetime. In order to reach his countrymen with the gospel, he traveled over 250,000 miles on horseback. His ministry produced lasting effects. Not only did he change the face of religion in England but, according to Woodrow Wilson, the course of English history. He opened new religious societies, administered discipline, raised vast sums of money for the poor, founded the first tract society, and engaged in controversy for the faith. At his death he left behind 135,000 communicants and five hundred preachers for the Methodist Church.

Wesley was born in 1703. In that same year, on the other side of the Atlantic, another man was born whose life greatly affected the church. Jonathan Edwards was a scholar. He was a child of a parsonage and was the grandson of Solomon Stoddard, a noted New England Puritan minister. Edwards possessed a brilliant mind. At six he mastered Latin; at nine he wrote a treatise on materialism; at twelve he produced an essay on spiders that is still considered biologically accurate. At thirteen he entered Yale, and at seventeen he graduated with highest honors.

Many of Edwards' sermons reflect his massive intellect. He wrote works on the *Freedom of the Will* and *A History of Redemption* that rank as classics of Christian theology. Just before his death at fifty-five, Jonathan Edwards accepted the presidency of Princeton College. His scholarship left a lasting impression on America. Barrett Wendell, a Unitarian literary critic, named Edwards as one of three outstanding thinkers that the United States has produced. Yale University has republished his works in honor of his contributions.

Both John Wesley and Jonathan Edwards were gifts from God to his church. The people of God need scholars who can think God's thoughts after him and evangelists who can proclaim that message clearly. If the church is to carry out Christ's commission, however, we need to go beyond a simple appreciation of both. We need a band of men and women who are theological evangelists and evangelistic theologians.

John Wesley and Jonathan Edwards combined both offices. As Wesley rode his 250,000 miles on horseback, he produced grammars of English, French, Latin, Greek, and Hebrew. He edited a Greek New Testament and made his own translation of the Bible. His sermons and journals contain the major planks of a systematic theology.

Jonathan Edwards, the scholar, became a major force in evangelism and revival. His sermon, "Sinners in the Hands of an Angry God," preached many times throughout New England, was the opening trumpet in the Great Awakening. His unrelenting logic, his identification with the feelings of his congregation, and his use of Scripture shook his hearers out of their complacency. Through him hundreds awoke to their desperate need of Jesus Christ.

Throughout history, effective evangelists have studied theology and strong theologians have involved themselves in evangelism. No one would question the zeal of the apostle Paul for evangelism. Under the inspiration of God he wrote to his friends in Rome, "I speak the truth in Christ—I lie not—I am ready to be anathema from Christ—to suffer eternal punishment and lose all that really matters to me—if only my people Israel could be saved!" Yet Paul was also a splendid theologian. Think of his letters to the Romans, the Ephesians, and the Galatians, and you marvel at the range and depth of his thought. His epistles written in the heat of his ministry are the quarry in which most subsequent Christian thinkers have been content to dig. In Paul theology and evangelism embraced each other. Paul became a theologian because he desired to evangelize, and theology formed the basis of his message.

Augustine, a theologian, shaped and directed Christian thought for centuries after him. But he wrote his greatest work, *The City of God*, motivated by a spirit of evangelism. When men and women despaired as they witnessed the collapse of Roman civilization, Augustine pointed them to the city whose builder and maker is God.

John Calvin stands out as one of the most successful evangelists in church history. This brilliant theologian not only evangelized the city of Geneva and the cantons of French-speaking Switzerland; he also became an "evangelist of Europe," spreading the evangelical faith from Scotland to Transylvania. Five times during his lifetime he revised his *Institutes of the Christian Religion* to achieve a clearer, more convincing explanation of Christian theology in order that his followers could be more effective evangelists.

William Carey, the pioneer of modern overseas missions, carried the burden of Christless millions heavy on his heart. While he longed to bring the gospel to the world, his brethren operating out of a stifling theology were inclined to do nothing. For that reason Carey set himself, while still a country pastor, to learn Hebrew, Greek, Dutch, French, and Italian. Then, driven by his concern for the lost, he traveled to India, where he lapped up language after language exploring the richness of Indian literature and still more sharing the treasures of Christ in the gospel. Carey established a publishing house and founded a great college, the first of its kind in India and a center of theological education on the subcontinent.

Francis Schaeffer challenged the assumptions of thousands of men and women caught up in the ferment of our times. While exposing the futility of pagan philosophy, he argued for the sufficiency of biblical truth as a foundation for life. Schaeffer, however, considered himself an evangelist whose major purpose in life lay in bringing bewildered people to a knowledge of the Savior.

Certainly there are scholars who lack spiritual fire, but that is not the fault of theology. Men and women like that would be deadly dull no matter what they did. Superficiality is not a necessary part of evangelism and, in fact, clear theology is basic to sound witness.

The Aims of the Evangelist

The first aim of an evangelist is to proclaim to the world the good news about Jesus Christ. Obviously that requires an understanding of the message. What does it mean "to believe on the Lord Jesus Christ"? Is that the same as saying, "Let Jesus come into your heart," "Open your life to Christ," or "Make Jesus Lord of your life"? If we read the sentence, "The blood of Jesus Christ, God's Son, cleanses us from all sin," what does that mean to the individual in the marketplace? How do you explain that truth in terms unchurched people comprehend? Take that biblical assertion apart and you are working with theology.

Sometimes what we call deep is simply muddy. Only if we understand the gospel ourselves can we hope to make it clear to others. Theology clarifies our thought, sets what Christians believe in contrast with false doctrine, and helps us make the message clear to outsiders.

A second purpose of the evangelist is to help converts develop into mature Christians. People professing faith in Christ often do not stand because they do not grow. Only the strong meat of Christian doctrine produces healthy Christians, and we never get very far as Christians without first understanding the great truths revealed to us by God in Scripture and then in faith applying them to life.

If theology is basic to evangelism, evangelism is vital to theology. God's truth demands proclamation as well as study. If we propose to be Christians, then we must be on with Christ's business. Napoleon's lieutenants carried in their jackets, close to their hearts, a map of the world. World conquest was their purpose because it was Napoleon's purpose. For that they fought, sacrificed, suffered, and died. Christian scholarship exists to serve Christ's people in the world. There is a story about Jerome, the scholar who translated the Scriptures into Latin. He was a theologian and philosopher, a grammarian who mastered Hebrew, Greek, and Latin. Like all students Jerome loved his books. In his sleep one night he dreamed he stood before the judgment seat of Christ.

"Who are you?" said the Lord on the throne.

"Jerome, a Christian," was the reply.

"That is false," said the stern voice from the throne.

"You are not a lover of Christ, but of Cicero, for where your treasure is, there your heart is also!"

Jerome awoke in a cold sweat and fell to his knees to beg forgiveness for being so in love with his manuscripts that he forgot the men and women for whom Christ died.

As much as we love books we must love Christ and people more. The evangelist needs the scholar, and the scholar needs the evangelist. Even more, the church needs scholarly evangelists and evangelistic scholars—men and women who love God not only with heart and soul but with mind as well.

C. I. Scofield was a noted pastor in Dallas, Texas, and the original editor of the *Scofield Bible*. During the year 1918 he suffered a serious illness that gave him an opportunity to evaluate his ministry. In January of 1919 at the opening of a new year he wrote a letter to many of the Bible teachers he knew. One of those to whom he wrote was William Pettingill. This is what Scofield wrote.

> Dear and Honored Brother:
> You and I are Bible teachers. It is of God's grace, and it is a great gift. But near to it is a great danger.
> For many months I have, through physical disability been laid aside from all oral ministry. During this time it has been increasingly laid upon me that I should beg the forbearance of my teaching brethren while I state in plain truth the teacher's danger.
> In a word, it is the neglect of the Gospel message to the unsaved. But, brother, *that* is the *great* message. It is sweet and needful to feed the flock of Christ, but it is to seek and save lost men and women that Jesus came, died, and rose again. It is not enough to repeat Gospel texts and say, "Come to Jesus." There is a *tender* seeking note in the gospel truly preached. How many gospel sermons did you preach in 1918? How many found salvation under your ministry? Let us make 1919 a mighty, tireless effort to save lost men.
> Yours in Christ's love,
C. I. Scofield

We can resolve to do the same thing. If we cannot be scholarly evangelists, then by God's grace let us determine to be evangelistic scholars.

 uestions to Consider

1. What is the nature of the antagonism between theology and evangelism?

2. How did figures like John Wesley and Jonathan Edwards deal with theology and evangelism?
3. What are the issues you deal with as you consider theology and evangelism?
4. In what ways can you become a better theologian and a better evangelist?
5. How do you respond to Haddon Robinson's suggestions for dealing with the antagonism between theology and evangelism?

Bookshelf

Douglas, J. D., ed. *The Work of an Evangelist*. Minneapolis: World Wide Publications, 1984.

Gresham, Charles, and Keith Keeran. *Evangelistic Preaching*. Joplin, Mo.: College Press, 1991.

Loscalzo, Craig A. *Evangelistic Preaching that Connects*. Downers Grove: InterVarsity Press, 1995.

McLaughlin, Raymond W. *The Ethics of Persuasive Preaching*. Grand Rapids: Baker, 1979.

Mounce, Robert. *The Essential Nature of New Testament Preaching*. Grand Rapids: Eerdmans, 1960.

What Authority Do We Have Anymore?

I attend a Bible study with business executives, and recently one man commented that in all the years he had been in business, his pastor had never visited him at his office.

"It's just as well," said another. "A minister would feel out of place in my office."

Since I consider myself a minister, I pressed him to explain.

"Most ministers I know come across best visiting those in the hospital or working in church environs. That's their turf." He went on to say that he saw the world of the pastor and the world of business people as very different. "The pastor is used to working alone or with a small staff, and his interest is relationships. The world of business is a more impersonal atmosphere, dominated by people who put an emphasis on the bottom line.

"Pastors do pretty well with issues of grief and loneliness and interpersonal ethics—not stealing, coveting, fornicating, and so on," he said. "But I don't know too many pastors who address the problems of the individual's conflicting loyalties in groups and organizations."

Another man, who helps run a large construction corporation, agreed and offered an example: "A fellow owed us $500,000

29

when he died. He and his wife owned a house that was worth $150,000. The question is, do we sue the estate for the money we're due, even if it costs the woman her house as part of the payment for her husband's debt?"

He continued, "If you own the company, you can make a compassionate decision if you want to. But when you're responsible to stockholders, and your job is to collect bad debts, where is your higher loyalty? Now, you might argue, '$150,000 isn't worth it.' But suppose the house is worth $500,000? Now do you go after it? Or a million? Is it ethical to go after a $500,000 house but unethical to go after a $150,000 house?"

The businessmen agreed—rarely in church do they hear anybody even mention these kinds of issues. And yet that's the common stuff of life. Those tough, morally ambiguous issues are where some business people have to live out their faith.

"While the preacher talks about absolutes, right and wrong," one man said, "most of us deal with gray situations."

Another said, "My pastor talks about 'the good being an enemy of God's best,' but people in my world aren't dealing with first or second moral choices. They're down to the twelfth or thirteenth choices.

"As much as I appreciate my pastor and enjoy his sermons," the businessman concluded, "it's not often that he speaks about my world."

I was dismayed by the conversation. Not everyone would agree with these businessmen; some people attend church expecting their minister to say something that will help them understand the broad issues of life a little better. But not many expect the preacher to be able to speak with insight to the particular world in which many of them live.

Changing Times

Time has changed the way people view pastors. The average preacher today is not going to make it on the basis of the dignity of his position.

A century ago, the pastor was looked to as the person of wisdom and integrity in the community. Authority lay in the office of pastor. The minister was the parson, often the best-educated person in town and the one to whom people looked for help in interpreting the outside world. He had the unique opportunity to read and study and often was the principal voice in deciding how the community should react in any moral or religious situation.

But today, the average citizen takes a different view of pastors and preachers. Perhaps we're not lumped with scam artists or manipulative fund raisers, but we face an Olympic challenge to earn respect, credibility, and authority.

In the face of society's scorn—or being relegated to a box labeled "private" and "spiritual"—many preachers struggle with the issue of authority. Why should anyone pay attention to us? What is the source of our credibility? In such a climate, how can we regain the legitimate authority our preaching needs to communicate the gospel with power and effect?

Let me identify six guidelines that have assisted me.

Articulate Unexpressed Feelings

One way to build credibility with today's congregations is to let people see that you understand their situation. Many people in the pew suspect that preachers inhabit another world. Folks in the pew may listen politely to a reporter of the distant, biblical past, but they won't be gripped unless they believe this speaker speaks to their condition.

This is why, in a sermon, I try to speak for the people before I speak to them. Have you ever listened to a speaker and found yourself saying, "Yeah, that's right; that's my reaction, too"? The speaker gave words to your feelings—perhaps better than you could have expressed them yourself. You sensed the preacher knew you. He explained you to you.

We capture the attention of people when we show that our experience overlaps theirs. For instance, a preacher might say, "There's no good place for a .150 hitter in a championship lineup. No matter where you put him, he's out of place." If listeners know sports, they know that's true. The preacher's speaking their language.

Or the minister may take a punch line from a comic strip, or use material from *Business Week* or *Advertising Age* or *The Wall Street Journal*. A business executive will resonate with that. Obviously this pastor knows a bit more about the bottom line than playing Monopoly. Through illustrations, the preacher has revealed something about his reading, his thinking, and awareness of life. When some areas of a speaker's life overlap with the listeners', they are more likely to listen. He's gained some credibility. An ingredient in effective preaching is using specific material that connects with lives in the congregation.

Listen to the Invisible Congregation

Another way effective preachers connect with the audience is to sit six or seven specific flesh-and-blood people around their desks as they prepare. I have assembled such a committee in my mind as real to me as if they were there.

In that group sits a friend who is an outspoken cynic. As I think through my material, I sometimes can hear him sigh, "You've got to be kidding, Robinson. That's pious junk food. What world are you living in?"

Another is an older woman who is a simple believer, who takes preachers and preaching very seriously. While I prepare sermons, I ask, "Am I raising questions that will trouble her? Will my sermon help her?"

A teenager sprawls in the circle, wondering how long I'm going to preach. I can make the sermon seem shorter if I can keep him interested.

A divorced mother takes her place feeling alone and overwhelmed by her situation. What do I say to her?

Those are four of my seven. Another is an unbeliever who doesn't understand religious jargon and yet has come to church but doesn't quite know why. Another makes his living as a dock worker. He has a strong allegiance to his union, thinks management is a rip off, curses if he gets upset, and enjoys bowling on Thursday night.

The last is a black teacher who would rather attend a black church but comes to a white church because her husband thinks it's good for their kids. She is a believer, but she's angry about life. She's very sensitive about racist remarks, put-downs of women, and will let me know if my sermon centers on white, middle-class values dressed up as biblical absolutes.

I change the group from time to time. But all of them are people I know. They have names, faces, and voices. I could prepare a vita on each of them. While they do not know it, each of them contributes significantly to my sermon preparation.

Admit Complexity

Let's face it. Life is complex. We sometimes preach as though it were not.

One time after I'd preached a sermon on love, a man came up and said, "You said that love means always seeking other people's highest good."

"Yes."

"That's fine, but my business puts me in competition with another man in this congregation. I run an efficient operation that lets me sell my product cheaper than his. What's the loving thing to do—underprice him and take some of his customers? Or should I keep my prices roughly equal?"

Before I could respond, he went on.

"But that's not the toughest part. A large corporation has just moved into town selling the same product. I'm going to have to scramble to stay in business myself. I may have to cut prices so drastically it will drive my fellow church member into bankruptcy.

"I want to love this man. We're in the same Sunday school class. I coach his kids in Little League. I want to do what's best for him. But the name of the game out there is survival," he said. "Why don't preachers talk about these kinds of things when they talk about love?"

For us to communicate with authority, we've got to step into the shoes of those Christians who are in the home and marketplace. No matter how gray the issues, we've got to be willing to say, "As a pastor, I must talk about the hard questions." In our preaching, we must recognize the complexity of the issues. How do we do that?

First, it's helpful simply to admit the tension and point it out. All truth exists in tension—God's love exists in tension with his holiness. Skillfully applying love and justice is not easy.

I believe God honors an honest try. People need to know that. Sometimes I'll point out that we will make a wrong decision with the right motive, which is very different from making a right decision out of a wrong motive. As far as I know, the Bible never calls any action, in itself, right. No action is right apart from its motive. Obviously, there are some acts the Bible calls wrong: murder, lying, adultery. But it's not as easy to classify right behavior.

Jesus talks about two men who went to the temple to pray—which sounds like a good religious act—except one is justified, and the other is not. Jesus talks about people giving—and that's a good thing—except some give to be seen by others. That's not good.

So in God's economy, motive is a key factor. One of the things we preachers can say with authority to people is: "In these situations, it's important to handle life skillfully, to make the right decisions. But the prior and more important decision is What's motivating you? Are you willing to be God's representative in this situation? Are you seeking what's best in the lives of the people involved? Sometimes those decisions are confusing. We need wisdom. That's what Christian friends and Christian counsel give you."

Speak with Authority

Preachers, of course, have to be more than "fellow strugglers." No one is helped by "You're a loser; I'm a loser; let's keep losing together."

People want to believe you have taken your own advice and, while you've not arrived, you're on the way. You'll never learn to be a .300 hitter by watching three .100 hitters. You study a .325 hitter. Although he will occasionally strike out, he knows how to hit.

Likewise, people want to listen to somebody who knows what the struggle is, has taken the Bible's message seriously, and knows how to hit.

Of course, we identify with the needs and experiences of our people—we're every bit as human as they are. But our task is to speak a word that is qualitatively different from normal conversation. Effective preaching combines the two and gives people hope that they can be better than they are.

When the combination is right, we preach with authority, which is different from being an authoritarian. Preaching with authority means you've done your homework. You know your people's struggles and hurts. But you also know the Bible and theology. You can explain the Bible clearly. Preachers aren't being authoritarian when they point people to the Bible. When Billy Graham explains, "The Bible says . . ." he's relying not on his own authority but on another—God's Word—and he shows how that authority makes sense. We help our credibility when we practice biblical preaching.

The authoritarian, on the other hand, is someone who speaks about biblical and nonbiblical things in the same tone of voice. Whether the subject is the Super Bowl or the Second Coming, the verdict is delivered with the same certainty and conviction.

I realized the distinction one night when my wife, Bonnie, said to me, "You've been around the Bible too much. Any opinion from politics to sports has the same ring as your sermon on Galatians." It's easy to fall into that. An authoritative tone without genuine biblical authority is sound and fury signifying nothing.

When we speak with authority, we preach the Bible's message without embarrassment, but we also communicate that we don't always know how to tailor faith to life.

Be Precise in Descriptions

Authority also comes from a track record of being truthful and not distorting the facts. It's especially important to be precise in our definitions and descriptions, whether we're defining the historical background of the text or delivering an apt illustration. Accuracy builds credibility.

I once used an illustration about snakes and referred to them as "slimy, poisonous creatures." A woman came up afterward and said, "Snakes aren't slimy; they are dry. And most snakes aren't poisonous." She worked in a zoo, so she spotted that I was careless in my description. As a result, I had given her reason for suspecting the rest of what I had to say.

The need for precision is particularly acute with an antagonistic or less than supportive audience. They'll focus on your minor error as a reason for not listening to the rest of what you have to say.

With the high stakes involved, what do we say when we need to use an illustration from an area outside our expertise? The answer lies in a recent sermon I heard. The preacher was from Britain, and he was trying to identify with his American audience by talking about baseball. He referred to a "four-base hit." Baseball fans know you don't get a four-base hit—it's a homer. That didn't turn me off to the sermon, but I remember thinking, 'He doesn't know baseball.' It distanced us. His credibility was diminished.

He could have sidestepped the difficulty had he simply admitted, "Look, I'm a stranger to baseball, but I enjoyed watching it. As I saw the game, here's what happened." Then people understand the speaker isn't trying to speak with authority on this issue, and they grant him or her the license to speak in less-than-precise terms.

Years ago when I first began to teach at Dallas Seminary, I asked Charles Ryrie, another a professor on the faculty, if he had any advice to help a young professor. He replied, "Whenever you state the case of someone disagreeing with you, imagine that your opponent is sitting in the front row of the class.

State his position in such a way that he would say, 'Yes, that is what I believe.' And then you can take issue with the position."

The advice for the classroom is good advice for the pulpit. It is dishonest to characterize someone else's position in a way that person would disavow. Being precise and fair, even with differing viewpoints, also adds to our credibility.

Display Character

For church leaders, perhaps no factor contributes more to legitimate authority and credibility than authentic Christian character. It's what Aristotle called ethos; in New Testament terms, it's being mature, upright. It's what you are, which is always more important than what you do. These days, if we want credibility in the pulpit, genuine character has to come through.

The difficulty, however, is that credibility comes from the way people perceive a pastor's character, and this may or may not align with what the pastor really is. Some pastors, dedicated to Christ and to the ministry, present themselves in a way that disguises their true character. A male pastor may be courageous but be perceived as effeminate. Another may have deep convictions but come across as slovenly or boring. How people perceive our character, spiritual life, intellectual life, and family life has much to do with how they respond to our ministry.

Part of effective preaching is the ability to make the presentation match the internal conviction. The image we project will influence our credibility. Appearance in the pulpit will affect the way people respond. I'm convinced inwardly, for example, of the importance of discipline and order in the Christian life. How can I present myself in a way that matches the conviction? In the first thirty seconds, people are deciding whether they're going to listen. God looks on the heart, but people in our culture look on the outside. Am I disheveled? Do my shoes need to be shined? If I'm fifty pounds overweight, they may perceive that I'm not disciplined or that I'm careless about myself.

Obviously one advantage of a lengthy ministry is that the pastor has a better chance to bring perception and reality together. The long-term pastor is judged more on his pattern of behavior than on a specific appearance. People are more likely to say, "The pastor not only talks love; he gives love. He was there in our family crisis when we needed him." A pattern of care can cover a multitude of less-than-stellar sermons.

Of course, the flip side is that we may have things to live down, and that also takes time. A pastor I know lost his temper in a board meeting and spoke some harsh words in anger. Now, months later, when he stands in the pulpit, some people play that record mentally. Another pastor in a similar situation confessed his misuse of anger and publicly asked for forgiveness. He got it. In his case, people learned that the fellow they saw in the pulpit was real and had integrity.

 Questions to Consider

1. How has time changed the way people view pastors?
2. How can a preacher capture the unexpressed feelings of his or her listeners?
3. Who are the six or seven people you will place around your desk each week as you prepare your sermon?
4. What advantage is there in admitting and pointing out the tension in a passage?
5. In what way does character influence preaching? How important is it?

Bookshelf

Craddock, Fred B. *Overhearing the Gospel.* Nashville: Abingdon, 1978.

Dodd, C. H. *The Apostolic Preaching and Its Developments.* 1936. Reprint. Grand Rapids: Baker, 1980.

Jabusch, Willard F. *The Person in the Pulpit: Preaching as Caring.* Nashville: Abingdon, 1980.

Luccock, Halford E. *In the Minister's Workshop.* 1944. Reprint. Grand Rapids: Baker 1976.

Stott, John R. W. *The Preacher's Portrait.* Grand Rapids: Eerdmans, 1961.

A Profile of the American Clergyman

Heretics make headlines. When a minister publicly denies the cardinal beliefs of his church, it's news. If she openly supports a lesbian lifestyle, reporters know that sells newspapers. But what about the clergy whose names appear only in the Saturday church announcements? What do they believe? What kinds of lifestyles do they approve? What do they feel about the ministry or the social-ethical issues of our day?

A modern business axiom proclaims, "In God we trust—all others must have data." To gather data to answer these questions, *Christianity Today* employed the Gallup organization and its affiliate, the Princeton Religious Research Center, to survey American clergy. A group of 1,060 Protestant ministers, selected at random, took time to answer 45 questions sent to them in the mail. In a separate sample, 998 Roman Catholic clergy also filled out the questionnaire. The denominational proportion of Protestant clergy participating in the survey corresponds to the actual number of clergy in the various denominations. Baptists made up 17 percent of the respondents; Methodists 14 percent; Lutherans 12 percent; Presbyterians 9 percent; United Church of Christ 4 percent; Episcopalians 3 percent; and the Christian Church (Disciples of Christ) 2 percent. Other religious bodies represented in the sample—Mormons, Eastern Orthodox, Bible churches, to name a few—each made up 1 percent or less of the total.

According to the study, most Protestant clergy serve relatively small congregations. Only 12 percent reported an active membership of 1,000 or more, while over half said they pastored churches with less than 300. Congregations that call their minister "the preacher" have support from the clergy: when asked what they considered the most important activities of pastoral ministry, 56 percent of the ministers singled out preaching. The closest second, checked by 15 percent of the respondents, was administration of the sacraments. That does not necessarily mean that clergy feel their preaching is effective. When asked, "What programs in your church are especially successful?" less than 10 percent mentioned preaching. About a third selected "liturgy—worship services." Among evangelicals, youth ministries topped the list.

Clergy Beliefs

American clergy tend to classify themselves as theologically conservative rather than liberal. Over half—53 percent—declare they are evangelical. Over 20 percent say they are fundamentalists. One-third answer to "traditional confessional." Ten percent accept the label "charismatic." Only 15 percent of the clergy characterize themselves as "liberal" and 8 percent as "neo-orthodox." Within the evangelicals, 55 percent regard themselves as philosophically conservative compared to 37 percent who see themselves as "middle of the road" or a small 6 percent who think of themselves as "liberal." What is more, members of the clergy believe their congregations view them as they view themselves.

Conservative doctrinal positions emerge again and again throughout the survey. Seven in ten ministers believe "the Bible is the Word of God and is not mistaken in its statements and teachings." Among evangelicals, over 95 percent accept that position. Clergy under 30 are more likely to hold this view of Scripture than their elders. In fact, throughout the study, young persons in the clergy appear more traditional and theologically conservative than their older colleagues. As many Catholics hold this high view of the Bible as Protestants. Catholics and Protestants differ significantly, however, when it comes to testing religious beliefs. While 76 percent of Protestants cite the Bible as their chief authority, 77 percent of Catholics say they test their beliefs "by what the church says." On questions about the person of Christ, respondents were even more orthodox. The great majority of clergy (87 percent) believe that "Jesus Christ is fully God and fully man." Catholics are virtually unanimous in this doctrinal affirmation. Approached negatively, only 1 percent of all the clergy accept the proposition, "Jesus Christ is not God or the Son of God, but was a great religious teacher." The only significant deviation from the strong affirmation of Christ's deity and humanity came from Methodists: 30 percent felt that "Jesus Christ was a man, but was divine in the sense that God worked through him. He was the Son of God."

Ninety-nine percent of both Protestant and Catholic ministers believe in life after death and eight out of ten go on to affirm that "the only hope for heaven is through personal faith in Jesus Christ." A basic issue of the Reformation still separates Protestants and Catholics, however: 61 percent of Roman Catholic clergy believe that "heaven is a divine reward for those who earn it by their good life."

Continuing the conservative trend, a strong majority of clergy believe that the devil is a personal being. Catholics, Southern Baptists, and those over 50 are more likely to affirm this than others in the sample. Once again Methodists as a group file a minority report. About one in five maintain that the devil does not exist either as a person or a force for evil in people's lives.

In the face of pervasive teaching about evolution in our school systems, it is significant that 57 percent of the clergy and half of the general public still believe "God created Adam and Eve, which was the start of human life." Younger clergy are more likely to accept this than their elders. Catholics, however, differ with Protestants on this question. Two-thirds of Catholic clergy agreed with the statement, "God began an evolutionary cycle for all living things, including man, but personally intervened in a point in time and transformed man into a human being in his own image." Creation and evolution divide evangelicals. "Liberal" evangelicals appear much more likely to adopt an evolutionary position than those who characterize themselves as "conservative" or "middle of the road."

Eight out of ten clergy testify to having had a "religious experience," but the experience relates to some degree to their religious affiliation. For instance, Protestants are more likely than Catholics to have had such an experience, and Baptists are twice as likely as Lutherans. Within the group reporting a religious experience, better than nine out of ten said it involved Jesus Christ, and three out of four saw it as a turning point that included asking Jesus Christ to be their personal Savior. While most of those who report a religious experience feel it continues to hold significance for them, among Catholics and Lutherans the experience is not usually associated with conversion.

The Emphasis on the Individual

What about the personal lives of the clergy? Press reports of pastors and priests leaving the ministry make it appear that large numbers pick up their cross only to drop it along the way. According to the survey, however, only about three in ten indicated they "often" or "occasionally" considered leaving the ministry. Just as many replied that they have "never" considered dropping out. Catholics are less likely than others to have flirted with this possibility. In their personal lives, about half of the clergy feel they live up to their own moral and ethical standards most of the time. About one in three admit that while they try to live up to their standards, they find it difficult. However, few felt their standards were impossible to maintain. When temptation does assault the clergy, it is not blamed on the society around them. Only 2 percent checked the response "there is so much in today's culture that works against my standards that I often find it impossible to live up to what I think is right." Alcohol poses less of a threat to ministers than it does to the general public. While two out of three lay persons drink, less than half of the clergy indulge. Among evangelicals, three out of four are total abstainers.

Do clergy regard the world as their parish, or the parish as their world? On the one hand, when asked which pastoral activity gave them "least satisfaction," 28 percent said "community service" (ranking under administration, which received the lowest marks of all). Yet, most agreed that "helping win the world for Jesus Christ" should hold top priority for a Christian. While Methodists and liberals are less likely to affirm that priority, it still ranks as the dominant opinion in these two groups as well. Two out of three respondents say the church should concentrate more on personal than social renewal; the remaining third vote for equal emphasis. Only 2 percent favor making social renewal the primary concern of the church. These reactions stem from a strategy embraced by four out of five ministers—personal renewal generally leads to social renewal. Even among liberals, the response stands four to one that if we renew persons we can renew society.

This emphasis on the individual does not necessarily imply the church has no business in politics. Three out of four of those questioned believe that religious organizations should take a public position on what they feel to be the will of God in political-economic matters. Catholics hold this more often than Protestants and young adults seem somewhat less likely to opt for political expression than their elders. The clergy also respond in impressive numbers that "religious organizations should try to persuade senators and representatives to enact legislation they would like to see become law."

If the clergy should decide to get together on political-economic issues, though, they could not agree on what legislation to push. What could be expected is that the clergy would generally be more conservative than the public at large. For example, only 3 percent of the clergy agree that abortion is "acceptable under any circumstance," while 13 percent of the public accept that statement. After that the clergy split. While over 80 percent of the Protestants feel that abortion is "acceptable under only certain circumstances," only a quarter of the Catholics assent to that. Most insist that abortion is unacceptable in all circumstances.

Sexual Issues and Society

A heavy majority (84 percent) believe sexual relations before marriage are wrong—while only half of the general public see that as true. Catholic clergy hold this view more often than Protestants, but conservative and middle-of-the-road evangelicals hold it even more strongly than Catholics. Among liberals, however, one out of four accept the idea that premarital sex may be right. When it comes to extramarital sex, the clergy present a more unified front—96 percent declare that an extramarital affair is wrong.

Homosexuality, another issue of our times, does not get such widespread denunciation. While eight out of ten clergy across the nation reject homosexual relations between consenting adults as sinful (Southern Baptists and conservative evangelicals hold this unanimously), among theological liberals better than one out of four disagree.

The clergy also appear more conservative than the public on divorce. The dominant position of ministers is that "divorce should be avoided except in an extreme situation." On the other hand, the dominant view of the public is that "divorce is painful, but preferable to maintaining an unhappy marriage." On this issue Catholic and Protestant clergy stand together. The strictest view on divorce is held by ministers under 30. Almost one out of five feel that "divorce should be avoided under any circumstances."

What about remarriage after divorce? In the population at large, one out of three persons feel that "remarriage after divorce is always acceptable," but only one out of ten clergymen agree with that statement. Thirty-seven percent prefer the alternative "remarriage after divorce is acceptable if reconciliation to the former mate is not possible, regardless of the reason." Surprisingly, 22 percent of Catholic clergy endorse that position.

When asked what should be done about poverty in their community, two out of ten members of the public felt no obligation beyond paying taxes. Another two believed they should try to persuade church and government organizations to aid the poor. Three more were willing to contribute to such organizations. Only two out of ten felt they should be involved personally and directly. Members of the clergy contrast sharply with the public. One-third believed they should personally be involved with the poor, while an additional third felt a responsibility to persuade church, religious, and government agencies to help. Almost as many believed they should contribute to religious and community groups. Less than 1 percent of the ministers in the country felt that paying taxes alone was enough. More impressive, according to their answers, clergy involve themselves with the poor far more often than do the general public. They work personally with the poor, contribute to agencies that assist the poor, and persuade others to get involved. While 27 percent of the public confess they have done nothing about poverty in their community, only 1 percent of the ministers make such an admission.

Conclusion

Clearly, the *Christianity Today*–Gallup Poll and members of the press don't pose identical pictures of the American clergy. Ministers as a group hold much more conservative positions on theological and ethical questions than a newspaper reader might suspect. Nor do ministers live in steeples high above the pavement. In impressive numbers, they get involved at a personal level with needy men and women around them.

In the months and years to come this broad survey will be broken out into its separate parts and the thinking and actions of the clergy will be analyzed in detail. Through these studies church leaders today and historians of the future will have an accurate understanding of where ministers positioned themselves as the decade began.

Questions to Consider

1. In what ways do you think clergy beliefs affect one's preaching?
2. How do some of the current cultural teachings conflict with your belief system? How do you deal with them in your preaching?
3. What does the emphasis on the individual mean to preaching?
4. What are the issues you face as you consider the sexual and social concerns Robinson discusses?
5. How do you think you would have responded had you been questioned by the poll?

Bookshelf

Hansen, David. *The Art of Pastoring: Ministry Without All the Answers.* Downers Grove: InterVarsity, 1994.

Packer, J. I. *A Quest for Godliness.* Wheaton: Crossway Books, 1990.

Peterson, Eugene H. *The Contemplative Pastor.* Carol Stream: Leadership/Word Books, 1989.

Swetland, Kenneth L. *The Hidden World of the Pastor: Case Studies on Personal Issues of Real Pastors.* Grand Rapids: Baker, 1995.

Willard, Dallas. *The Spirit of the Disciplines: Understanding How God Changes Lives.* San Francisco: Harper, 1988.

Preaching with a Limp

When I was president of Denver Seminary, the school was hit with three lawsuits in the late 1980s. In one case, a former student had sexually molested a boy, and the family sued the seminary. Two others involved a former professor who had gotten inappropriately involved with a counselee.

For one of the cases, I had to give a deposition. I had no idea what to expect, but I wasn't worried because neither I nor the seminary had done anything improper. With our lawyer at my side, I walked into the room where the deposition would take place, where we met four lawyers from the prosecution.

The questioning began, and I quickly came to a frightening realization. The four lawyers across the table were ruthless, and my lawyer wasn't prepared. This was the first time he had handled such a case. They were wolves, and he was a lamb. Neither one of us was ready for what happens at a deposition.

Only later did I learn the legal strategy behind such depositions. The prosecution knows that even if you are innocent, lawsuits can bring financial ruin. Insurance companies are wary of juries, and they stand to pay out $100,000 even if you win your case. So they're often willing to settle out of court regardless of guilt or innocence.

All the action, then, takes place in the depositions. That's where the prosecution tries to intimidate you, expose your vulnerability, and make you want to settle out of court. In my case, they did a good job.

My deposition lasted two days. The first day prosecution lawyers grilled me for nine hours with question after question, doing everything they could to cast my answers into a negative light, twisting my motives, questioning my integrity.

Since then I have talked to others who have endured a deposition, and they have said it was the worst experience of their lives. It certainly was for me.

But that was only the beginning. The seminary's insurance company at one point said I personally wasn't covered by the school's policy. (I was also named in the suit.) At one point, my lawyer (my new lawyer!) said, "They don't have a good case against us." But he knew that in this day anything can happen in court, so ten minutes later he advised, "You ought to take all your assets and put them in your wife's name."

"Will that protect them?" I asked.

"No. They can still get them, but it makes it harder."

So our retirement savings all went in Bonnie's name.

Meanwhile, a former employee of the school began to spread untruths about me throughout the community, which damaged my reputation. I had no effective way to respond.

The pain Bonnie and I suffered during those months was devastating. Frankly, I didn't respond well. Like the apostle Paul, I struggled with "conflicts on the outside, and fears within."

And yet I had to keep preaching, at chapel, in conventions and churches where I had been scheduled for months in advance, and later as interim pastor at Grace Chapel in Massachusetts.

All pastors go through times when they must preach through pain. How do you preach when you don't feel like it—when you're distracted, unable to focus, when your family is in turmoil or your health is failing or detractors in the church are launching artillery rounds in your direction, when you're going through loneliness or feelings of failure?

Dangers in the Tunnel

Going through extended times of pain feels like walking a dark, damp tunnel. The tunnel of a preacher's pain has some unique dangers.

First, we can end up using the pulpit for self-therapy. One's style of preaching can change during a crisis. Often, along the way, a suffering pastor preaches a sermon that is nine-tenths his painful story and one-tenth Bible. Listeners identify with the sermon and are moved.

The pastor hears a favorable response to the message, and the next week, because it's difficult to study at such a time, he decides once again to share from his heart. The message is based primarily on his experience, with a sprinkling of Scripture thrown in. Again listeners respond warmly.

Soon he sets a pattern. He is now in danger of preaching weekly from his experience rather than from the Bible. Instead of experiencing what he preaches, he is preaching what he experiences. Preaching becomes a catharsis for his pain.

You cannot make the pulpit a place for self-therapy very often without paying a penalty. Parishioners don't come to church every Sunday to hear the wrestlings of the pastor's soul. They're not unsympathetic, but after a while the weekly service becomes an emotional downer. People don't follow for long leaders who can't handle their emotions.

Another danger is using the pulpit as a sniper's perch. If our pain comes from a church conflict, the temptation is strong to use the pulpit to draw a bead on opponents.

Let's say Deacon Bill Jones is out to get the pastor. In the sermon the pastor quotes the verse "Alexander the metalworker did me a great deal of harm."

"We all know what this is like," the pastor says. "There will be times when we want to go forward for God, and others will stand up in a business meeting and call the congregation back to the past. We need to follow God as did the apostle Paul, even when others try to block our way."

The pastor never mentions Bill Jones, but anyone in the know sees right through the comments. They'll be upset that the pastor used the pulpit as a weapon, especially if they feel Deacon Jones's opposition has merit.

If our church is in conflict, we have to take care that people can't read into our comments an attack we never intended.

Furthermore, we can fail to preach the full counsel of God. When we're in pain, we tend to think everyone is in pain. Even if we never mention our personal troubles, our preaching can become strictly an ambulance service focused on crises. Those who are healthy, moving up in their businesses, and feeling strong in the Lord, won't get much out of our preaching.

I went with my daughter to the movie *Wall Street* several years ago. Gordon Gecko, one of the key characters in the film, was a successful, even ruthless, player of the stock market.

After the movie, my daughter said, "Daddy, what if Gecko said to you, 'You're a Christian. What can you say to somebody like me? You have one hour to give me your best shot.' What would you say to him?"

She gave me pause. Sometimes the church doesn't know what to say to the Gordon Geckos of the world. We can only speak to them, it seems, after they have fallen. Yet, the Scriptures speak both to the weak and the strong. I don't intentionally ignore successful people in sermons, but that's easy to do when I'm in pain.

When we're suffering, we need others to remind us there are more preaching themes than depravity, grace, faith, and prayer. We need to preach also about righteousness, God's sovereignty, justice, outreach, and other fundamental doctrines. Just because some themes aren't feeding me at the moment doesn't mean they no longer are good food for others.

Preaching in the Dark

Some painful situations are naturally shared with the congregation: the death of a loved one, serious illness.

Other situations require discretion: financial problems, marital stress, conflict on the board, a moral lapse. Even if we never mention such problems, our preaching changes as we walk the tunnel of pain.

As I was living through this intense period of pain at Denver Seminary, several people said they sensed more tenderness and sympathy in my preaching. That is certainly what I felt. If anything good for me came out of this painful time, it was the overwhelming sense of my need of God. I felt completely vulnerable. Although I was not guilty of any legal negligence or failure, I felt more in need of grace than ever.

When prosecutors hammered away at my motives and conduct, when others spread slander and rumors, it forced me to examine my life. I looked into my heart and saw that in spite of my legal innocence, I was like every other person, a sinful human being with impure motives much of the time, in need of God's grace all the time.

One sermon I preached while "in the tunnel" was the parable of the Prodigal Son. I talked about the Father: not worrying about his dignity, his heart filled with grace and acceptance, he ran to meet his son, the prodigal. "I just want you to know the Father is running to meet you," I told the congregation. "His arms are open wide, and he's not angry with you. More than anything else, he just wants you to come home. He says, 'I don't care if you're covered with mud and manure. I don't care how you smell. Welcome home! Welcome home!'

"If that's where you are this morning, I want to welcome you home. Come up here, and let me welcome you home."

One woman answering that appeal told me, "I've been in church and heard invitations all my life. There is no way in the world I would go forward in a church. But I wanted to come. I wanted to be welcomed home."

During a conversation with a work associate, I shared the ideas from that sermon, and she began to weep. She is a fairly controlled person. "Never in my life," she said, "have I felt the full meaning of that parable."

Such reactions weren't due to any new preaching technique or profound insight on my part. I had experienced God's grace anew, and the power of that grace simply came through, without my consciously striving for it to happen.

Pain and the Pastor's Family

Our families share the darkness when we walk through pain. They see us at our best and worst. And then they see us stand before a congregation and preach the will of God. Our families won't question our sincerity if we avoid two mistakes.

First, don't imply that what ought to be actually is in your life. A preacher's responsibility is to declare what Christians ought to do. We teach others to read their Bibles and pray daily, have family devotions regularly, share their faith at every opportunity, pray for our nation's leaders, give as much as possible to missions, sacrifice for others, live unselfishly. At the same time, few if any pastors do all that Christians ought to do.

That's no surprise and no problem, if we're honest. It's only a problem if we imply otherwise. And it becomes a major problem if we have pain in the family.

If we suggest in our preaching that we have all the answers, that our faith is unshakable, that "all you need is Jesus," that we have it all together, and meanwhile our family sees us in doubt, anger, and confusion at home, they'll conclude we are hypocrites and doubt the reality of what we preach.

When I went through my experience at Denver, I was not a model of unwavering, unquestioning faith. I went through times of deep discouragement. My family saw me go through those times. If I had stood up Sunday after Sunday and said, "When you go through a trial, put your faith in God. Don't waver. Don't doubt," I would have lost a lot of credibility with them.

Better to say something like, "When we go through trials, we need to put our faith in God. At times we may waver. At times we may doubt. But we need to pursue faith. Only by faith in the Lord Jesus Christ can we keep our footing when we feel we're slipping."

Second, don't illustrate with your best moments and imply that's the norm. For several months, a pastor suffers unrelenting attacks from his elder board. It gets the best of him. Embittered, he comes home each night and at dinner complains to his family about the latest criticism and speaks disparagingly about various board members.

One night in the middle of the conflict, by contrast, he says to the family, "We need to pray for the board members and their families. No doubt they have pain in their lives that is causing them to be negative toward me."

The next day and for weeks to come, however, the pastor falls back into bitter comments when with the family.

Later the pastor preaches on praying for enemies and illustrates by saying, "As you may know, we went through some disagreements here at the church several months ago. During that time God helped my family to sit together at the dinner table and pray for those who had personally attacked us."

He's telling the truth, but he's implying that the ideal was the norm. He probably isn't intentionally trying to mislead the congregation; he's trying to inspire them with an example of doing what is right. But he is in danger of embittering his family, who have seen his ambivalent behavior.

When You Don't Feel Like It

Pain makes it hard to concentrate on anything but our problems. It distracts us, confuses us, and saps our energies, leaving us feeling like we don't want to prepare sermons or get "up" for preaching. Preaching through pain requires that we do two things: compartmentalize and filter.

When we go through extended pain, we will often have to preach about things we don't resonate with at the time. We will talk about the sovereignty of God when we feel everything is out of control, or about confidence in God when we ourselves are struggling with unanswered prayer.

At those times, we need to fulfill the calling to preach the Bible. We preach what the Bible says, not what we feel. We, on our own authority, based on our own experiences, may not be able to say, "All things work together for good," but we can say, "God's Word says that all things work together for good."

In a sense, sometimes we have to compartmentalize our experience and feelings. At those times, we may not interact personally with the text or illustrate from our own lives. That's reality.

At such times, it's appropriate to recognize publicly the ambivalence between the text's great promise and the human condition. If you're preaching through the Psalms and come to a place where the psalmist says, "The Lord has rewarded me for my integrity, for the cleanness of my hands in his sight," but you feel the weight of your sin, you can say: "Perhaps you feel like the psalmist today. You're not perfect, but you're forgiven, and you're trying by his grace to walk with God. You feel like praising God that he is a God of justice who rewards the righteous and repays the wicked. You can do that. Others of you will feel a great sense of failure—I know I often do. You can't say with integrity, 'I've served you with my whole heart.' You're feeling instead like the 'chief of sinners.' So this psalm doesn't express how you're feeling today. Still, the psalmist is at a place all of us want to be at times. So let's all listen in, and see what we can learn."

We also need to filter. If we always keep a sermon "out there," we eventually lose our sense of authenticity. If we just keep hammering together what I call "dog house" sermons—Let's see, I need three points that begin with the letter T—without living in those sermons, we get hollow. On occasion we need to filter our preaching through our experiences, choosing sermon texts that resonate with what we feel, sharing some of the tough lessons we are learning even if we never tell the story behind them.

In years past, when I would read the parable of the sheep and the goats at the judgment, I felt like a sheep. I had faith in Christ; I visited friends in the hospital; I gave to World Vision.

When I went through the tunnel, I felt totally unworthy of salvation. For the first time, I read that parable and noticed that after Christ commended the sheep, they responded, "Who, me?" They didn't know they were sheep. They didn't feel like sheep.

I came to the conclusion that if I get into heaven, it's because God says I'm a sheep, not because I feel like I'm doing what sheep do. It's all grace.

I began preaching that passage. I felt I had to preach it because it reflected my heart; it made some sense of what I was going through.

After the three lawsuits against Denver Seminary were settled, my lawyer met with the faculty to explain all he could not explain during the trials. He told the faculty, for example, that the president of another seminary had gone over all the testimony and seminary records. He testified that he would have handled the situations just as I had. After all the facts came out, some of the faculty contacted me to say that meeting had vindicated me.

The whole thing is behind me now, though my life will never be the same. And neither will my preaching.

Questions to Consider

1. When faced with difficulties in ministry, what are some of the issues preachers are tempted to preach about? What does Haddon Robinson suggest preachers focus on instead?
2. What is the family's role in preaching through pain?
3. How can the preacher check his or her motives when preparing to preach?
4. What are some of the dangers that preachers face when experiencing pain?
5. What difficulty are you currently facing in your ministry? How have you responded to it in your preaching?

ookshelf

Hicks, H. Beecher, Jr. *Preaching Through a Storm*. Grand Rapids: Zondervan, 1987.

Jeter, Joseph R., Jr. *Crisis Preaching: Personal and Public*. Nashville: Abingdon, 1998.

Lutzer, Erwin W. *Pastor to Pastor*. Grand Rapids: Kregel, 1998.

Massey, James Earl. *The Burdensome Joy of Preaching*. Nashville: Abingdon, 1996.

Rowell, Ed. *Preaching with Spiritual Passion*. Minneapolis: Bethany House, 1998.

The
Preacher
and Preaching

What Is Expository Preaching?

The church in the twentieth century desperately needs biblical preaching. However, not everyone agrees with that verdict. The word is out in some circles that preaching should be abandoned. The moving finger has passed it by, we are told, and it is now pointing to other methods and other ministries that are more "effective" and up to date.

To explain why preaching has been discredited would take us into every area of our common life. For one thing, the image of the preacher has changed. No longer is he or she regarded as the intellectual and spiritual leader in the community. Ask the man in the pew what a preacher is, and his description may not be flattering. Kyle Haselden is afraid that some people have an image of the preacher as "a bland composite which shows the pastor as the congregation's congenial, ever helpful, ever ready to help boy scout; as the darling of old ladies and as sufficiently reserved with the young ones; as the father image for young people and a companion to lonely men; as the affable glad hander at teas and civic club luncheons."[1]

In addition, preaching has lost support because it takes place in an overcommunicated society which bombards us with a hundred thousand "messages" a day. Television and radio feature pitchmen delivering "a word from the sponsor" with all the sincerity of the evangelist. In that context a preacher may sound like another salesman who, in Ruskin's words, "plays stage tricks with the doctrines of life and death."

Add to these reasons the reality that liberalism has robbed the person in the pulpit of an authoritative message. Fads in communication have become more important than truth. Multimedia presentations, films, videos, sharing sessions, colored lights, and modern music may be symptoms of either health or disease. Certainly, modern methods can enhance communication, but often they are used because there is no message at all—and the unusual somehow masks the vacuum.

Then too, action appeals to us more than talk and listening. "Stop preaching at me" we say, and that reveals our irritation with preaching. Preaching in some churches is regarded as little more than a "necessary evil" that goes with being a Christian. People with this attitude may conclude the apostles had things backward when they observed, "It is not right that we should forsake the Word of God to serve tables." In our day of activism, there is a temptation to declare, "It is not right that we should forsake the service of tables to preach the Word of God."

Taking Scripture Seriously

No one who takes the Scriptures seriously, however, dares to count preaching out. Paul was a writer. From his pen we have the inspired letters of the New Testament. Heading the list of his writings is his Epistle to the Romans. Measured by its impact upon history, few documents can compare with it. But when Paul wrote this letter to the congregation in Rome, he confessed, "I long to see you, that I may impart to you some spiritual gift to strengthen you, that is, that we may be mutually encouraged by each other's faith, both yours and mine" (1:11–12). Some ministries cannot take place apart from face-to-face contact. Even the writing of an inspired letter is not a substitute. "I am eager to preach the gospel to you who are in Rome" (1:15). Power exists in the word spoken that the written word cannot replace.

Preaching in the minds of the New Testament writers is God in action. Peter, for example, reminded his readers that they had "been born anew, not of perishable seed but of imperishable, through the living and abiding word of God" (1 Pet. 1:23). How did this word come to do its work in their lives? "That word," Peter explains, was "the good news which was *preached* to you." Through preaching they were redeemed.

Paul wrote of the Thessalonians that "they turned to God from idols, to serve the living and true God, and to wait for his son from heaven" (1 Thess. 1:9–10). This "about face" occurred, says the apostle, because "when you received the Word of God which you heard from us, you accepted it not as the word of men but as what it actually is, the Word of God, which is at work in you believers" (1 Thess. 2:13). Preaching, therefore, was not merely talk about God. It was God Himself working through the message and personality of the preacher confronting men and women and bringing them to Himself.

This explains why in 2 Timothy 4:2 Paul encourages his young associate Timothy to "preach the word." The word for "preach" means "to cry out, herald, or exhort." It is as though the message should so stir a person that it must be poured out with passion and fervor. Not all passionate pleading from the pulpit, however, has divine authority. While a preacher must be a "herald"—he or she must herald the Word. Anything less cannot legitimately be called "preaching."

The constant temptation of the preacher is to cry out some other message than the Scriptures—a political system, a theory of economics, a new religious philosophy. No matter that this may be done in authoritative tones, if a preacher does not preach the Scriptures he abandons his authority. He no longer confronts men or women with the Word of God but simply speaks another word from a man.

God speaks through the Scriptures to all people in all times. The Bible is not merely "the old, old story" of what God did in some other time and place, nor is it only a statement of ideas about God—inspired and inerrant. The Bible is God's tool of communication through which He addresses men and women today. Through the Scriptures, God brings us to salvation (2 Tim. 3:15) and to a richness and ripeness of Christian character (2 Tim. 3:16–17).

Defining Expository Preaching

The type of preaching that most effectively lays open the Bible so that people are confronted by its truth is expository preaching. At its best, expository preaching is "the communication of a biblical concept, derived from and transmitted through a historical, grammatical, and literary study of a passage in its context, which the Holy Spirit applies first to the personality and experience of the preacher, then through him or her to the listeners."

This definition has several parts. First of all, the substance of the expository sermon is derived from the Scriptures. The expositor realizes that although the Bible is a book like no other book, it is still a book. In fact, it is a collection of writings which can be studied like other literature. R. A. Montgomery, in his book *Expository Preaching*, makes this point: "The preacher undertakes the presentation of particular books (of the Bible) as some men would undertake the latest best seller. The preacher seeks to bring the message of definite units of God's word to his people. He discovers the main theme or constituent parts of the book's message as they were in the mind of the writer . . . His treatment of words, phrases, texts, portions is important not only for what they may say separately, but as they relate to the main theme of the writer and the end he had in view in writing this book."[2]

In a larger sense, therefore, expository preaching is more a philosophy than a method. It is the answer to a basic question: "Does the preacher subject his thought to the Scriptures, or does he subject the Scriptures to his thought?" Is the passage used like the national anthem at a football game—it gets things started but then is not heard again? Or is the text the essence of the sermon to be exposed to the people?

Though it is possible to preach an orthodox sermon without explaining a biblical passage, unfolding a portion of Scripture guards the preacher's thought against heresy. Doing this regularly, it forces the preacher to speak to the many issues of life dealt with in the Scriptures that he otherwise might easily overlook. Above all, the preacher speaks with an authority not his or her own, and the person in the pew will have a better chance to hear God speak to him or her directly.

A second important factor in the definition involves the means by which the biblical message is communicated to the congregation. The preacher transmits it on the same basis by which he or she received it. In the study, the expositor examines the grammar, history, and context of the passage. In the pulpit, the preacher must deal with enough of the language, background, and setting of the text so that an attentive listener is able to check the message from the Bible.

As a result, effective expository preaching will be occupied largely with the explanation of Scripture. A good expository sermon will reflect the passage not only in its central message, but also in its development, purpose, and mood. As this takes place, people not only learn the Bible as they listen, they are also stimulated to study the Scriptures for themselves.

Benefits of Expository Preaching

Expository preaching offers great benefits to the preacher. For one thing, it gives the preacher truth to preach. Many ministers spend a frustrating part of their week "starting to get underway to begin" their sermon preparation. Only a genius can think up enough original material that is fresh and stimulating and that will keep the same audience interested one hundred times a year. The person who draws topics from his own mind and experience dabbles in a puddle. The man or woman who expounds the Scripture does business in great waters.

Expository preaching provides the preacher with many types of sermons. A single verse may be expounded (Alexander McLaren was outstanding in this respect). A passage may be expounded—this is what is usually considered as expository preaching. In addition, he may trace a topic or doctrine through the Bible. To do this, the preacher finds the many places in which a topic or doctrine is considered. First, the topic is related to the particular passage in which it is found, then it is related to the other passages. Biographical preaching may also be expository. Much of the Scripture comes to us in the form of history or biography. If six men are taken out of Genesis, for example, there is not much left.

Our definition tells us that expository preaching also develops the preacher into a mature Christian. When an expositor studies the Bible, the Holy Spirit probes the preacher's life. As a preacher prepares sermons, God prepares the person. Alexander McLaren said that everything he was, he owed to the fact that day after day he studied the Scriptures. As the expositor masters a passage, he or she will discover that the truth of that passage in the hand of the Spirit who masters him or her. P. T. Forsyth understood this when he wrote: "The Bible is the supreme preacher to the preacher."[3]

The Purpose of Expository Preaching

Finally, the basic purpose of expository preaching is the basic purpose of the Bible. It takes place so that through it the Holy Spirit may change people's lives and destinies. Preaching and teaching, of course, are not the only means by which God builds His people, but they are His major means. The effective expositor knows that God is not speaking to men today about the Bible as though it were a textbook in history or archaeology. The Holy Spirit speaks to men and women today about themselves from the Bible. The person in the pulpit or those in the pew do not sit in judgment on Judas, or David, or Peter, or Solomon. Under the teaching of Scripture, they must judge themselves.

To carry out this purpose the expositor must not only know the message, but the people to which it will be delivered. She must exegete both the Scriptures and her congregation. Imagine that Paul's letters to the Corinthians had gotten lost in the mails and had reached the Christians in Philippi instead. Those people would have been perplexed at what Paul wrote. The believers in Philippi lived in different situations than their brethren at Corinth. The letters of the New Testament, like the prophecies of the Old Testament, were addressed to specific people living in particular situations.

"Doctrines must be preached practically, and duties doctrinally," was the way our Protestant forebears put it. Perhaps this is the largest problem in what is called "expository preaching" today. The preacher lectures about the "there and then" as though God lived back in the "once upon a time," and he fails to bring the eternal truth to focus on the attitudes and actions of people in the "here and now." Application is not incidental to effective expository preaching, it is crucial!

In relating the Bible to experience, however, the expositor dares not twist the Scriptures to fit people's lives. Instead he calls men and women to bring themselves into subjection to the standards of the Bible. Christians must conform to the age to come, not to this present age. The application moves both ways. Biblical truth must be related to people's lives; but on the other hand, people's lives must be changed to be relevant to biblical faith.

Conclusion

F. B. Meyer, himself a gifted expositor, understood the awe with which a biblical preacher approaches his task: "He is in line of great succession. The reformers, the Puritans, the pastors of the Pilgrim fathers were essentially expositors. They did not announce their own particular opinions, which might be a matter of private interpretation or doubtful disposition; but, taking their stand on Scripture, drove home their message with irresistible effect with, 'Thus said the Lord!'"[4]

The major problems of our society are ultimately spiritual. Men and women always stand in desperate need of God. "They will not ask for help, unless they believe in Him, and they will not believe in Him unless they have heard of Him, and they will not hear of Him unless they get a preacher, and they will never have a preacher unless one is sent. But as the Scripture says the footsteps of those who bring good news is a welcome sound . . . So faith comes from what is preached, and what is preached comes from the Word of Christ" (Rom. 10:14–17, The New Jerusalem Bible).

 ## Questions to Consider

1. What does it mean to discover the subject of a passage?
 2. How does Haddon Robinson use the term *complement* and what does he mean by it?
3. How is an idea of a passage formed?
4. What is the significance of biblical preaching?

Bookshelf

Forsyth, P. T. *Positive Preaching and the Modern Mind.* London and New York: Independent, 1907.

Haselden, Kyle. *The Urgency of Preaching.* New York: Harper & Row, 1963.

Meyer, F. B. *Expository Preaching Plans and Methods.* 1910; Grand Rapids: Zondervan, 1954.

Montgomery, R. A. *Expository Preaching.* New York: Fleming H. Revell, 1939.

Stott, John R. W. *Between Two Worlds: The Art of Preaching in the Twentieth Century.* Grand Rapids: Eerdmans, 1982.

Homiletics and Hermeneutics

Once upon a time an explorer discovered an ancient sundial. Realizing its value, he chipped away the dirt accumulated on its face and restored it to its original condition. He then placed the sundial in a museum where it would be shielded from the elements—including the sun. Although he valued the instrument, he did not use it. Evangelicals sometimes resemble that explorer with his sundial. What they prize in theology, they ignore in preaching.

Homiletics deals with the construction and communication of sermons. As a communicator, the preacher borrows from rhetoric, the social sciences, and communication theories. Yet because he handles religious content, he must also involve himself with hermeneutics. A homiletician, therefore, cannot merely ask, "How do I get the message across?" He must also ask, "How do I get the message?"

Men and women who believe the Bible to be the Word of God without error insist, "You find your message in the Scriptures." If we regard the Bible as God's tool of communication through which He addresses people in history, then it follows that preaching must be based on it. Expository preaching, therefore, emerges not merely as a type of sermon—one among many— but as the theological outgrowth of a high view of inspiration. Expository preaching then originates as a philosophy rather than a method. It reflects a preacher's honest effort to submit

69

his thought to the Bible rather than to subject the Bible to his thought.

Not all preaching from evangelical pulpits, however, finds it source in the Bible. Declaring to a congregation that the Bible is God's Word—even in a sweaty voice—does not mean that it is expounded. Nor does all preaching or orthodoxy necessarily build on a biblical base. Ministers often repeat "the old, old story" without taking a fresh look at the Bible or without demonstrating to a thoughtful hearer that what they proclaim does indeed come from the Scriptures.

Expository Preaching

When preachers announce a text they sometimes practice sleight of mind—now you see it, now you don't. The passage and the sermon may be nothing more than strangers passing in the pulpit. Yet, it is a rape of the pulpit to ignore or avoid in the sermon what the passage teaches. Topical preaching common in American pulpits flirts with heresy. Deuteronomy 18:20 warned that the prophet who spoke in the name of God what God had not spoken should be executed.

Admittedly, sound doctrine can be taught without referring to specific biblical passages, but grounding one's sermons in Scripture protects a preacher from error. More positively, through expository preaching a minister speaks with authority beyond his own and those who sit before him have a better chance of hearing God address them directly. An expositor possesses confidence that his message is not "the word of men," but that "It really is the Word of God, which also performs its work in you who believe" (1 Thess. 2:13).

What this means in practical terms is that the concepts set forth in the sermon must have their source in the Scriptures. At its heart, this is a moral matter. In the ancient world the herald not only had to possess a powerful voice, but qualities of character as well. Hauch Friedrich observes:

In many cases heralds are very garrulous and inclined to exaggerate. They are thus in danger of giving false news. It is demanded then that they deliver their message as it is given to them. The essential point about the report which they give is that it does not originate with them. Behind it stands a higher power. The herald does not express his own views. He is the spokesman for his master. . . . Heralds adopt the mind of those who commission them and act with the plenipotentiary authority of their masters . . . Being only the mouth of his master, he must not falsify the message entrusted to him by additions of his own.[1]

Expository sermons are derived from and transmitted through a study of a passage (or passages) in context. Not only should an expositor find the substance of his or her sermon in the Bible, but she communicates it to her hearers on the basis by which she received it. As he studies, therefore, the preacher wrestles with exegesis and hermeneutics—the materials of grammar, history, literary forms, the thought and cultural settings of his text. In the pulpit he deals with enough of the language, background, and context of his passage so that an attentive listener can follow the message from the Bible. The proper response to biblical preaching does not lie in pronouncing the pastor a skilled communicator but rather in determining whether God has spoken and whether or not He will be trusted and obeyed.

Expository Preaching Reflects Exegesis and Hermeneutics

Since effective expository preaching deals largely with the explanation and application of Scripture, it reflects exegesis and hermeneutics on every hand. For one thing, the theme of the sermon should develop from the thought of the Bible. While this sounds like keen insight into the obvious, it is observed more often in the breach than in the keeping. Every Sunday ministers claiming high regard for the Scriptures preach on texts whose ideas they either do not understand or have not bothered to study.

As a case in point, scores of sermons on prayer have been based on the wording of Matthew 18:19 and 20. "Again I say to you, that if two of you agree on earth about anything that they may ask, it shall be done for them by My Father who is in heaven. For where two or three have gathered together in My name, there am I in the midst."[2] At first glance, Jesus endorses prayer offered in groups of two or three and promises that if Christians agree together about a prayer request somehow they bind the Father in heaven. Good sense, if nothing else, would drive us to scrutinize the context of those verses (If two or three Christian Dallas Cowboy fans agree to ask God for victory in an upcoming game and if a few Christians on the opposing team pray for a Cowboy defeat, which group is God bound to answer?).

Actually, Jesus' words here have little to do with the subject of prayer but instead with how sinning Christians should be restored. In the immediate context, the "two or three" does not refer to a small group prayer meeting but to the witnesses summoned in verse 16. "But if he (the sinning brother) does not listen to you, take one or two more with you, so that by the mouth of two or three witnesses every fact may be confirmed." All that Jesus says, therefore, applies to Christians dealing with someone who has sinned. The old maxim reminds us that "a text without its context becomes a pretext." In battling for the inspiration of individual words of Scripture we sometimes forget that words are merely "semantic markers for a field of meaning." Particular statements must be understood within the broader thought of which they are a part or what we teach may not be God's Word at all.

In fact, an emphasis on verbal inspiration sometimes lures a preacher into eisegesis and error. For instance sermons on "How to know the will of God" advance the thesis that "Inward peace gives assurance of God's direction in our decisions." Colossians 3:15, "And let the peace of Christ rule in your hearts," is offered in support of that idea. Since every word of Scripture is God-breathed, the preacher provides a word study of *braxzeo* "to rule" or "to umpire." Christ's peace, the sermon goes, serves as a referee who "calls" each decision we make. When a Christian lives within God's will, he experiences peace which "surpasses all comprehension." Through this peace the referee, Christ, affirms our correct decisions. Should Christians make wrong choices, they will experience inner anxiety—a sign that they have stepped out of God's will.

Such an approach has the ring of exposition. It focuses on the Greek text and sounds extremely practical. Unfortunately it is not biblical. A reading of the context reveals that Paul is not talking about decision making, but instead about how Christians should relate to one another. T. K. Abbott comments that the phrase *peace of Christ* "is not to inward peace of the soul, but to peace with one another as the context shows." Using Colossians 3:15 to preach on God's guidance ignores completely the idea the apostle intended. When sermons proceed from such a cavalier handling of the Bible, they divorce sound hermeneutics from homiletics.

The common practice of using a single verse or fragment of a verse as a "text" can be blamed for leading many preachers away from the intended meaning of the biblical writer. For instance, many ministers calling people back to God, to the foundations of faith or to a lost morality, have posed the question found in Psalm 11:3, "If the foundations are destroyed what can the righteous do?" The question appears rhetorical. Without the foundations the righteous can do nothing at all. Yet, the question apparently comes from friends who speak as enemies of God. They ask in desperation, "If the foundations are destroyed what can the righteous do but give up?" In the second half of the psalm, however, David replies that righteous men and women have splendid options open to them. Their faith does not depend upon foundations but instead upon the sovereign God who judges both the wicked and the righteous. While sermons taking off from the question in verse 3 may offer stirring pleas to secure the foundations both in the church and society, they are not biblical. In fact, such preaching proceeds from a methodology that itself undermines the foundation of biblical thought.

R. W. Dale in his lectures on preaching told of a minister in England preparing a sermon on a verse he imagined was in the Book of Proverbs. Before leaving for the church on Sunday morning he decided to look up the exact reference. Upon leafing through the Proverbs he could not find his text. In desperation he turned to his concordance but could not locate it there either. So when the moment came to start his sermon he began, "You will all remember, my friends, the words of the wisest of kings"—and then launched into his message. On the basis of this incident Dale offered this advice, "When you take a text be sure it is in the Bible"[3] to which we should add, when a preacher finds a statement in the Bible, he must be sure that what he or she declares the Bible to say, is what the Bible actually says. To fail to do so is to sacrifice hermeneutics for homiletics.

Determining the Idea

A concern for hermeneutics in determining the basic idea of a sermon is a matter of integrity. Over one hundred years ago Nathaniel J. Burton spoke to all who propose to represent God when he asked in his Yale Lectures on Preaching:

> What is slander? Well, one form of it is reporting that a man has said something that he did not say. And why is not the Bible slandered when some inaccurate and unexegetical fumbler spends hours every week in public discoursings on what the Bible says? So then, our very veracity forces us to philology, to exegesis, to profound interpretation. If we intentionally misrepresent meanings, we are liars, plain as day. But if we misrepresent meanings through carelessness, or through laziness, it shows that we have in us the making of a liar. We are willing to make statement after statement that we have never taken the trouble to verify.[4]

Biblical preaching should not only be true to the Bible in its central ideas but in the development of those ideas as well. Many sermons that begin in the Bible stray from it in their structures. Homiletical methods sometimes tempt the minister to impose an arrangement of thought on a text foreign to that of the inspired writer. The shoe must not tell the foot how to grow. To be truly biblical, the major assertions supporting the sermon's basic concept must also be taken from the passage on which it is based. Of course, a preacher may sometimes rearrange his material along psychological lines, but whatever outline the sermon assumes—and this can vary with the audience, speaker, or occasion—its content should reflect the argument of the biblical author and ought at every place to be controlled by the writer's thought.

As a case in point, in Philippians 3:13–14 Paul sums up the passage that begins at verse 1. "But one thing I do: forgetting what lies behind and reaching forward to what lies ahead, I press on toward the goal for the prize of the upward call of God in Christ Jesus." During the previous twelve verses Paul argues that "the overwhelming value of knowing Christ and having his righteousness makes every other value worthless and worth surrendering." One common development of the major idea in this passage takes off on what things should be given up for the sake of knowing Christ. Usually such values as power, possessions, position, passions, receive mention. In the passage itself, however, Paul refers to none of those indulgences. It is doubtful whether such things ever proved much of a problem to Saul the Pharisee. What the apostle abandoned for the sake of Christ were advantages that provided spiritual status—his knowledge and obedience to the law, a zeal for God's cause, his heritage, and his religious discipline. Paul turned his back on the self-effort and self-esteem of legalistic righteousness to gain a completely different kind of righteousness, one that comes through faith and identification with Jesus Christ.

The apostle's development of thought differs markedly from popular handlings of these paragraphs. As a consequence, the preacher not only loses the power of a great biblical theme, settling for something closer to platitudes, but more basic, homiletics wanders off from exegesis and accurate hermeneutics. If God superintended the writing of Scripture and protected its details, then biblical preaching must reflect God's thought both in theme and development. Should a minister protest that such sermons suffer from a variety deficiency, he might discover that submitting his thought to the biblical author can produce vitality that no other homiletical method can offer. Donald Miller addresses himself to this when he writes:

> Someone has remarked that the Bible is not marvelous for the number of its ideas, but for the infinite variety of ways in which it presents a few very great ideas. To reflect the Bible's own variety in successive sermons would, in most cases, be a more effective savior from monotony than the efforts of the preacher's own individuality.[5]

Establishing a Purpose

A sermon constructed out of honest exegesis and sound hermeneutics will also be true to the Bible in its purpose. In theory, at least, every sermon has a purpose—the answer to the question, "Why am I preaching this sermon?" While the idea of the sermon is the truth to be presented, the purpose describes what the truth is intended to accomplish. A statement of purpose recognizes that truth exists not as an end in itself but as an instrument through which men and women establish a relationship with God and one another. A biblical sermon finds its purpose not merely in a study of the audience but primarily through exegesis and hermeneutics. Behind every section of the sacred writings lies the reason why the author included the material. In some books, the purpose is clearly stated (i.e., 1 Timothy 3:14–15; John 20:31) while in others the purpose must be discovered through a study of the broad sweep of the content. Preachers who honor the Bible will align the purposes of their sermons with the aims of the biblical writer.

An accurate interpretation of a book like Job requires that a minister determine the purpose of the writer. While the speeches of Job's friends are in the Word of God, they are not necessarily God's Word. Job's comforters offer many explanations for suffering—most of them half or three-quarter truths—yet at the conclusion of the book God declared them wrong. A sermon showing why those ancient counselors worked from an inadequate theology would be in line with the purpose of Job, but to handle their ideas and their development as though they uttered God's truth would ignore completely the aim of the book.

A less obvious but just as harmful way of ignoring the purpose of a biblical author lies in the common practice of employing the historical narratives as case studies in morals, virtues, or spiritual struggles. In such sermons the camaraderie between David and Jonathan models an ideal friendship which all Christians should imitate; the conversation of Jesus with the woman at the wellside provides lessons on personal evangelism; the story of Ruth and Naomi turns into an example of how Christians should relate to their in-laws; Jacob's struggle at Peniel demonstrates how one must wrestle with God for blessing; Nehemiah becomes a case book for leadership. What is not asked in these sermons is whether the biblical writer intended for these histories to be used in this manner.

The use of the Bible as a collection of examples springs from homiletics and the preacher's search for relevance in his sermon. When confronted with historical narrative the preacher has to ask, "What does this event from the long ago and far away have to do with God's people in the here and now?" One solution is to use the incidents as examples—either of good or evil—of virtues to be cultivated or evils to be avoided. Dwight Stevenson states the case this way:

> As superb literature the Bible is a mirror. Most of the men and women whom we see there are reflections. We can see ourselves mirrored there. The hearer of the sermon or reader of the Bible does not need to be smuggled into the passage. He is already there in the passage. This is possible because of the dynamics of psychological identification, such as that experienced by a spectator at a play with an actor on the stage, or that of a reader of a novel with its hero.[6]

This illustrative approach is reflected throughout modern American homiletical literature. Lloyd Perry speaks for the tradition in his *Manual for Biblical Preaching* when he writes about biographical sermons.

This is an excellent means of demonstrating the contemporary relevance of the Scriptures, for preaching on Bible characters gives the minister an opportunity to set forth in a clear fashion the modern counterpart to the experience of a biblical person. Furthermore, the use of this type of subject matter helps to make the Scriptures come alive with real persons who faced real situations, and with whose lives, difficulties, hopes, and relationships God was immediately concerned and intimately involved. A wealth of biblical material exists for the purpose of biographical preaching, and this type of subject matter also includes the possibility of bringing messages on the lives of men and women whose names are not found in the Scriptures but who lived for God and contributed much for the cause of his kingdom.[7]

The practice of using the historical narratives as examples is occasionally defended by using 1 Corinthians 10. In this chapter Paul recounts several episodes in the history of Israel and uses them to warn his readers in verse 6, "Now these occurred as examples, to keep us from setting our hearts on evil things as they did." Then after spelling out what the Corinthians should have learned from the experiences of their forefathers, Paul observes in verse 11, "These things happened to them as examples and were written down as warnings for us on whom the fulfillment of the ages has come."

Before homileticians can offer this passage as the biblical base for exemplary sermons, they must struggle with its exegesis. First, the Greek word *tupos* translated "example" does not mean "illustration" in the common use of that word. *Tupos* comes closer to the words "evidence" or "pattern." A *tupos* refers to an event in Israel's history that demonstrated how God deals with His people when they sin. God's working in that event shows how God keeps His promises. What is more, the event became part of Scripture to serve as a warning to the community of faith in every age. God creates the "typical" relationship and that explains why it "was written down."

Not only does the past event prefigure similar present or future events because God keeps His promises, but the emphasis in the Corinthian letter is that these events actually happened. In talking about an example, Paul does not mean that his readers should "see themselves in the story" but instead urges them to learn from what actually took place in sacred history. As Heinrich Miller puts it, "Against some supposed metaphysical interpretation, salvation history is interpreted as the self-fulfilling activity of God in concrete human history.[8] A *tupos*, therefore, lies closer to a "proof" or "model" than to an illustration or example that throws light on a truth.

Clearly, then, Paul must not be taken to justify introducing scriptural incidents into sermons to be used pictorially, pedagogically, or illustratively with the unstated assumption that they carry divine authority. While the Bible may serve as a source of illustration to explain or apply a point or to convince an audience that a proposition is valid, if the historical event is separated from its purpose, then it does not carry the weight of Scripture and examples from church history, modern literature, or the morning newspaper would serve as well. In fact, we could argue that modern nonbiblical illustrations might be more effective since they would more likely illustrate the unknown by the known and would not imply that stories from the Bible carry the force of inspiration.

When a preacher ignores the purpose of a passage when using an incident as the text of his sermon, he has no defense against liberal theology. If he uses the historical narrative in order to speak about the temptations and problems of men and women in the pew, he would do as well to put aside the biblical text rather than to draw illegitimate parallels not intended by the biblical author. Sidney Greidanus in his stimulating book *Sola Scriptura* states the matter this way:

> The *Sola Scriptura*, so ardently confessed in theory, barely functions in the practice of exemplary preaching: one hardly needs the Bible for exemplary sermons. Ironically, the exemplary preacher, earnestly toiling to portray the man in the text in his personal struggles, therewith the better to draw a line to

the man in the pew, could, methodologically, have saved himself the trouble and sketched merely the man in the pew, for
motivated by the search for analogy (relevance), he loses precisely that distinctiveness which occasioned the appearance in
the Bible of the man in the text.[9]

Obviously, a preacher must draw a parallel between the persons in the Scripture and the people in the pew. The objection
lies in unwarranted parallels that ignore the purpose of the passage in its historical context and draw authoritative principles
for living from one example.

Handling Historical Narrative Passages

How, then, can a preacher handle historical narrative passages so that they carry the authority of inspiration? First, he
must understand that the writers of Scripture do not pretend
to write with antiseptic detachment. They were not morally or
spiritually neutral. The historians of the Bible were theologians
and they wrote from a divine point of reference. The writers of
the four Gospels, for example, did not give us four chronolo-
gies of the life of Jesus. They were evangelists writing history
from a theological perspective. Narratives in both the Old and
New Testaments proclaim God's acts in history. Before a
preacher can deal with a particular passage, therefore, he must
look to the larger context of the book to ask why this writer
recorded this story for his particular audience. Until he can sit
where the biblical author sat as he addressed his readers, he
cannot determine the relevance of the book or any of its passages for Christians today. The purpose of the sermon must
flow out of the purpose of the historical narrative. We must
read the text as the first readers read it before we can read it
into the life-situations of people in the twentieth century.

This means that the preacher deals with the passages as parts
of the canon. While source studies may provide guidance to the
meaning of the text, he does not deal with the traditions or

"subtextual" sources. His primary concern is with the Scripture in its final, canonical form, for in the way the history is assembled the message is framed. As in any other kind of biblical literature, the narrative must be left in its own immediate and broad context. The preacher cannot clip the story from the page and move it around to suit his own purposes.[10]

The preacher finds the purpose of narration by studying the arrangement of materials and noticing editorial comments offered by the writer. For example, in recording David's affair with Bathsheba and his consequent murder of her husband, Uriah, the writer of Second Samuel tells us, "When Uriah's wife heard that her husband was dead, she mourned for him. After the time of the mourning was over, David had her brought to his house and she became his wife and bore him a son." At that point in the narrative, it might appear that David had protected his reputation by shrewdly covering up his sins. The historian, however, becomes a theologian when he adds, "But the thing that David had done displeased the Lord" (2 Samuel 11:27). In the pages that follow, the historian-theologian recounts a series of tragedies in David's family—Amnon rapes his half-sister, Tamar, and then in revenge is murdered by Absalom. Absalom, David's favorite son, rebels against his father and rapes David's concubines in public. Later Absalom meets death at the hand of Joab, the same general who arranged the killing of Uriah. All of them emerge as wages of David's disobedience. While the historian does not moralize, his editorial comments and the orderings of the incidents demonstrate his purpose—to show that forgiveness does not necessarily wipe out consequences, and God brought open punishment on what was done in secret.

The narrative of Eglon's victory over Israel and his grisly assassination by Ehud (Joshua 3) has been used as evidence that God approves of killing tyrants. Others see in the account the moral that all men are Ehuds and have murder in them. Yet, the author of Judges comments, "The Lord strengthened Eglon" (Judges 3:12) and again "the Lord raised up for them a deliverer, Ehud" (Judges 3:15). Clearly, the purpose of the historian was not to provide a case study of a political assassination but to demonstrate that God works through the Eglons and the Ehuds of the world to accomplish His purpose for His people in history.[11] Although the ethical element remains, it develops from the author's view of God and demonstrates that even shocking political intrigues are controlled by God.

All of this is to say that in expository preaching the idea, the development, and the purpose of the sermon must precede from proper exegesis and hermeneutics and then be directed to the church today. The minister must exegete the passage and the people. He must recognize what the people to whom he ministers have in common, and what they do not share, with God's men and women in the first century and the centuries beyond. Relevant application as well as accurate exegesis raise hermeneutical questions that must be solved.

The Mood of the Passage

Exegesis and hermeneutics should also be reflected in the sermon's mood. While the emotion of a writer may be more difficult to pin down than ideas and their development, every passage has a mood. The mood involves the feelings of the writer and also the emotions his writings evoke in the reader. Some passages are alive with hope, some warn, some create a sense of joy, some flash with anger at injustice, others surge with triumph. A true expository sermon should create in the listener the mood it produced in the reader. Marvin R. Vincent stated the case for mood this way:

> The expositor must . . . aim to put himself for the time into the very atmosphere and spirit of the age out of which the word comes; not only to know, but to feel the motives of its acts and sayings. He must catch the quality of Jacob's shrewdness; he must glow with Deborah's warlike ardor; he must appreciate the political sagacity, no less the fatherly tenderness of Jephthah; he must thrill, like the singers of the Pilgrim Psalm, with inspiring and mournful memories of Jerusalem; he must be touched with the grateful affection which overflows in Paul's letter to the Philippians, and burn with the righteous indignation of his words to the Galatians and Corinthians.[12]

The personality of the preacher must submit to the atmosphere and spirit of a passage. As a case in point, a sermon on the opening verses of Peter's first letter should radiate with praise to God for a Christian's living hope. Yet, a minister bent on scolding his congregation can create a mood of guilt by charging that his hearers lack this hope. While other passages may have a spirit of rebuke, this one does not, and to fail to ring the changes on thanksgiving and victory is to live in the atmosphere of a defeated church of today rather than of the apostles.

As there are dominant and supporting ideas in a passage so, especially in larger passages, major and minor moods occur. Yet, as there are controlling ideas so there are dominant moods. That dominant mood, at least, should mark the spirit of the sermon. While recreating the atmosphere requires thought, feeling, and skill, expository preachers need to be as true to the mood as to the message of the passage. The tasks of the poet, the playwright, the artist, the prophet, and the preacher overlap at this point—to make people feel and see. Peter Marshall described the challenge to the preacher this way:

> What we have to do is to take a passage of Scripture and so carefully and accurately reconstruct the context of it that the scene comes to life. We see it first ourselves. Then we take our listeners to the spot in imagination. We make them see and hear what happened so vividly that the passage will live forever in their minds and hearts. It is like a newsreel from the Scriptures . . . a film from the world's big drama.[13]

Conclusion

Exegesis, hermeneutics, and homiletics, therefore, link together as supporting disciplines. The biblical preacher builds bridges that span the gulf between the written Word of God and the minds of men and women. He must interpret the Scripture so accurately and plainly and apply it so truthfully that the truth crosses the bridge. In Paul's last letter to Timothy he urges Timothy to "cut straight" the Word of God. The Greek word *orthotomounta* was used of road making—the writers of the Septuagint used it in Proverbs 3:6: "He will make your paths straight." Exposition of the Scriptures should be so simple and direct, so easily followed that it resembles a straight road. To do that the minister as a good workman must be faithful to both the Bible and to his listeners, and in doing so will gain the approval of God.

Ɒuestions to Consider

1. According to Haddon Robinson, how are expository sermons determined?
2. What are the tensions between exegesis and hermeneutics?
3. How does the biblical author's development of thought inform the biblical preacher?
4. What is the role of the biblical author's purpose and the purpose of the sermon?
5. How does the mood of the biblical passage inform the mood of the sermon?

ookshelf

Chapell, Bryan. *Christ-Centered Preaching*. Grand Rapids: Baker, 1994.

Davis, H. Grady. *Design for Preaching*. Philadelphia: Fortress, 1958.

Greidanus, Sidney. *The Modern Preacher and the Ancient Text: Interpreting and Preaching Biblical Literature*. Grand Rapids: Eerdmans, 1988.

Long, Thomas G. *The Witness of Preaching*. Louisville: Westminster/John Knox, 1989.

Perry, Lloyd. *Biblical Preaching for Today's World*. Rev. ed. Chicago: Moody, 1990.

Blending Bible Content and Life Application

It was a disastrous sermon. A church in Dallas invited me to preach on John 14. That's not an easy passage. It is filled with exegetical questions about death and the Second Coming. How do you explain, "If I go and prepare a place for you, I will come again, and receive you unto myself"? How is Jesus preparing that place? Does Jesus mean we won't go to be with him until he comes back? What about soul sleep? I spent most of my week studying the text and reading the commentaries to answer questions like these.

When I got up to preach, I knew I had done my homework. Though the issues were tough, I had worked through them and was confident I was ready to deliver solid biblical teaching on the assigned passage.

Five minutes into the sermon, though, I knew I was in trouble. The people weren't with me. At the ten-minute mark, people were falling asleep. One man sitting near the front began to snore. Worse, he didn't disturb anyone! No one was listening.

Even today, whenever I talk about that morning, I still get an awful feeling in the pit of my stomach.

What went wrong? The problem was that I spent the whole sermon wrestling with the tough theological issues, issues that intrigued me. Everything I said was valid. It might have been strong stuff in a seminary classroom. But in that church, in that pulpit, it was a disaster.

What happened? I didn't speak to the life questions of my audience. I answered my questions, not theirs. Some of the men and women I spoke to that day were close to going home to be with the Lord. What they wanted to know was, "Will he toss me into some ditch of a grave, or will he take me safely home to the other side? When I get to heaven, what's there?"

They wanted to hear me say: "You know, Jesus said he was going to prepare a place for us. The Creator of the universe has been spending 2,000 years preparing a home for you. God only spent six days creating the world, and look at its beauty! Imagine, then, what the home he has been preparing for you must be like. When you come to the end of this life, that's what he'll have waiting for you."

That's what I should have preached. At least I should have l started with their questions. But I didn't.

If it's also possible to make the opposite error—to spend a whole sermon making practical applications without rooting them in Scripture. I don't want to minimize Scripture. It's possible to preach a skyscraper sermon—one story after another with nothing in between. Such sermons hold people's interest but give them no sense of the eternal. Talking about "mansions over the hilltop" comes from country-western music, not the Bible. A sermon full of nonbiblical speculations is ultimately unsatisfying.

Some of the work I did in my study, then, could have helped the people answer their questions. The job is to combine both biblical content and life application in an effective way.

How Much Content Is Enough?

How then can we strike the right balance in our preaching between biblical content and life application?

The basic principle is to give as much biblical information as the people need to understand the passage, and no more. Then move on to your application.

The distinction between exegesis and exposition is helpful here. Exegesis is the process of getting meaning from the text, often through noting the verb tense or where the word emphasis falls in the original languages. That's what you do in your study when you prepare. But it's seldom appropriate in a sermon on Sunday morning. In fact, an overuse of Greek or Hebrew can make us snobs. Using the jargon of my profession can come across as a put-down, a way of saying, "I know something you don't know." There's an arrogance about that that can create distance between me and the audience.

I served for ten years as a general director of the Christian Medical and Dental Society. Sometimes physicians would use technical medical terms when they talked with me, and I wouldn't know what they were talking about. Once I said to one of my friends, "I hope you don't talk to your patients as you do me, because I don't know the jargon. I'm an educated person. I just don't happen to be as educated in medicine as you are."

Do you know what he said to me? He replied, "Preachers do that in the pulpit all the time."

I did a lot of that when I first got out of seminary. I used my knowledge of Greek and Hebrew in the study and in the pulpit. One day a woman wounded me with a compliment: "I just love to hear you preach. In fact, when I see the insights you get from the original languages, I realize that my English Bible is hardly worth reading."

I went home asking myself, *What have I done? I'm trying to get people into their Bibles, but I've taken this lady out of hers.*

Spurgeon was right: the people in the marketplace cannot learn the language of the academy, so the people in the academy must learn the language of the marketplace. It's the pastor's job to translate.

While raw exegesis doesn't belong in a Sunday morning sermon, what does belong there is exposition. Exposition is drawing from your exegesis to give the people what they need to understand the passage. They don't need all you've done in exegesis, but they do need to see the framework, the flow of the passage. They should be able to come back to the passage a few weeks after you've preached on it, read it, and say, "Oh, I understand what it says."

Does this mean there is no place in the church for exegesis? Of course not. As you study, you may dig out all kinds of material that would help certain people who enjoy detailed Bible study. While including these tidbits in a sermon resembles distracting footnotes, this kind of technical teaching is appropriate for a classroom.

Some pastors I know preach on a passage on Sunday and then follow up with a detailed exegetical study with a smaller group of interested people on Wednesday night.

Donald Gray Barnhouse had an interesting way of handling this. He commented as he did the Scripture reading. He would pause as he read to talk briefly about the tense of a verb or what some expression meant. He'd take ten minutes just reading the Scripture. His Bible reading was based on his exegesis.

Even then Barnhouse did not show off. He didn't give his congregation lessons in ancient languages. He simply took time to amplify the passage based on his study so that his people could appreciate the flow and nuances of the thought of the biblical writer. Some folks attending Tenth Presbyterian Church for the first time heard the Bible reading and thought they had heard the sermon!

When Barnhouse got to his sermon he was able to concentrate on the message of that passage, its implications, its application, which is what makes a sermon a sermon.

The "So What?" of Preaching

All preaching involves a "so what?" A lecture on the archaeology of Egypt, as interesting as it might be, isn't a sermon. A sermon touches life. It demands practical application.

That practical application, though, need not always be spelled out. Imagine, for example, that you borrow my car and it has a flat. You call me up and say, "I've never changed a tire on a car like this. What do I do?"

I tell you how to find the spare, how to use the jack, where to find the key that unlocks the wire rim. Once I give you all the instructions, then do I say, "Now, I exhort you: change the tire"? No, you already want to get the car going. Because you already sense the need, you don't need exhortation. You simply need a clear explanation.

Some sermons are like that. Your people are wrestling with a certain passage of Scripture. They want to know what it means. Unless they understand the text, it's useless to apply it. They don't need exhortation; they need explanation. Their questions about the text must be answered.

You may not need to spell out practical application when you are dealing with basic theological issues—how we see God and ourselves and each other. For example, you might preach on Genesis 1, showing that it's not addressing issues of science so much as questions of theology: What is God like? You might spend time looking at the three groups of days—the first day is light, the fourth day is lights; the second day is sea and sky, the fifth day is fish and birds. Each day is followed by God's evaluation: "It was good." But after the creation of man, God observes, "It was very good."

Then you ask, "What do we learn about God?" We learn that God is good, that God has a purpose in creation. We learn that while every other living thing is made "after its own kind," man and woman are created in God's image. What does that say about people—the people we pray with and play with, the people we work with or who sleep on the streets?

The whole sermon may be an explanation with little direct application built into it. Of course, that doesn't mean there's no application. If at the close of this sermon someone realizes, That's *missing word?* a significant statement about who we are. There are no ordinary people. Every man and woman has special worth—when that really sinks in—it can make tremendous practical differences as it shapes how a person sees himself and other people.

Or take Romans 3. You might begin by raising in some practical way the question, "How does a person stand right before God?" Then you could lead your listeners through Paul's rather complex discussion of what it means to be justified by faith. If you do it well, when you are finished, people should say, "So that's how God remains righteous when he declares us righteous."

Obviously, this passage has great application. But it's so complex you probably couldn't go through Paul's argument and spell out in any detail many practical applications, too, in the same sermon. And that's okay. If they really understood the problem of lostness, the solution of salvation serves as a strong application.

We need to trust people to make some of their own practical applications. Some of the best growing I've done has taken place when a concept gripped me and I found myself constantly thinking: How could this apply in my life?

Of course, you do have knowledge your people don't possess, knowledge they expect you to have and share with them. But you can share that knowledge in a manner that doesn't talk down to a congregation, in a way that says, "If you were in my situation, you'd have access to the same information." If you feel you must make all the practical applications for your hearers, do their thinking for them, you underestimate their intelligence. You can dishonor your congregation if you tell them in effect, "You folks couldn't have figured out for yourselves how this applies."

For me, though, the greater danger lies in the opposite direction—in spending too much time on explanation and not going far enough into application. After preaching I've often come away feeling I should have shown them in a more specific way how to do this. It is difficult for our listeners to live by what they believe unless we answer the question "How?"

Real-Life Examples: Necessary but Dangerous

To make a principle come to life—to show how it can be applied—we need to give specific real-life examples, illustrations that say, "Here is how someone faced this problem, and this is what l happened with her." But as necessary as real-life examples are, they carry a danger.

Suppose, for example, that someone preaches on the principle of modesty. Should a Christian dress with modesty? The answer is yes. But how do you apply that? One preacher may say, "Well, any skirt that's above the knee is immodest." So, he ends up with a church full of knee-length people. In that church, one application of a principle has assumed all the force of the principle itself. That is the essence of legalism: giving to a specific application the force of the principle.

I have a friend who keeps a journal, and it works for him. But when he preaches about it, he makes it sound as though Christians who are not journaling can't be growing. Whenever you say, "If you're not doing this particular act, then you're not following this principle," that's legalism.

How, then, can you preach for practical application if every time you say, "This is how to apply this truth," you run the risk of promoting legalism? Let me answer with a couple of examples.

When my father was in his eighties, he came to live with us. After a while he grew senile, and his behavior became such that we could no longer keep him in our home. Because his erratic behavior endangered himself and our children, we had to put him in a nursing home. It cost me half my salary each month to keep him there. For eight years, until he died, I visited my dad almost every day. In eight years I never left that rest home without feeling somewhat guilty about his being there. I would have preferred to have had him in our home, but we could not care for him properly.

A few years later, my mother-in-law, who was dying of cancer, came to live with us in our home in Denver. It was a tough period in our marriage. I was trying to get settled as president of Denver Seminary. My wife, Bonnie, was up with her mother day and night. She somehow changed her mother's soiled bed six or seven times a day. For eighteen months, Bonnie took care of her in our home. When Mrs. Vick died, we had no regrets. We knew Bonnie had done everything she could to make her last months comfortable.

How should Christians care for their aging parents? Do you keep them in your home or do you place them in a nursing facility? There is no single Christian answer. It depends on your situation, your children, your resources, and your parents.

There is, though, a single guiding principle: we must honor our parents and act in love toward them. To make a Christian decision, you can't start with a selfish premise; you start by asking what is best for everyone involved. How you apply that principle in a given situation depends on a complex set of variables.

The way to avoid the trap of legalism, then, is to distinguish clearly between the biblical principle and its specific applications. One way to do this in preaching is to illustrate a principle with two or three varying examples, not just one, so you don't equate the principle with one particular way of applying it.

When our children were young, I lived under the idea that if we didn't have daily devotions with our children—a family altar—somehow we were failing God. The problem was, family devotions worked for other people, but although we tried all kinds of approaches, they never worked for us. Our children sat still for them on the outside but ran away from them on the inside. Yet we kept at them because I felt that a family altar was at the heart of a Christian family.

Then I realized that family devotions wasn't the principle but the application of a principle. The principle was that I needed to bring up my children to know and love God. I had mistakenly been giving to our family devotions the same imperative that belonged to the principle behind it.

We then came up with a different approach, one that worked for us. Our two children left for school at different times. Each morning before Vicki left, I would pray with her about the day, about what was coming up. A little later, Torrey and one of his friends came into my study, and we'd sit and pray for five minutes about what their day held.

That may not sound as satisfying in a sermon as saying we had devotions as a family at the breakfast table every morning, but for us it was an effective way to honor the principle. A preacher must make a clear distinction between the principle and its applications.

This is not to say, however, that a biblical principle must sound abstract and vague. Sometimes a preacher merely translates the principle into terms that a congregation understands.

In our American frontier days, there was a settlement in the west whose citizens were engaged in the lumber business. The town felt they wanted a church. They built a building and called a minister. The preacher moved into the settlement and initially was well received. Then one afternoon he happened to see some of his parishioners dragging some logs, which had been floated down the river from another village upstream, onto the bank. Each log was marked with the owner's stamp on one end. To his great distress, the minister saw his members pulling in the logs and sawing off the end where the telltale stamp appeared. The following Sunday he preached a strong sermon on the commandment "Thou shalt not steal." At the close of the service, his people lined up and offered enthusiastic congratulations. "Wonderful message, Pastor." "Mighty fine preaching." The response bothered him a great deal. So he went home to prepare his sermon for the following Sunday. He preached the same sermon but gave it a different ending: "And thou shalt not cut off the end of thy neighbor's logs." When he got through, the congregation ran him out of town.

It's possible to state the principle in terms the audience clearly understands.

"We" Preaching and "You" Preaching

Another way to view the relationship between explanation and application is to look at the pronouns each calls for. Good preachers identify with their hearers when they preach. All of us stand before God to hear what God's Word says to us. The Letter to the Hebrews says that the high priest was taken from among men to minister in the things pertaining to man. The high priest knew what it was to sin and to need forgiveness. With the people, he stood before God in need of cleansing. In identifying with the people, he represented the people to God.

But that same priest, by offering a sacrifice, could minister God's cleansing to the people. Not only did he represent the people to God, he also represented God to the people. Somehow, that's also what preaching does.

When I'm listening to a good sermon, there comes a point when I lose track of all the people around me. As the preacher speaks, I experience God talking to me about me. The time for explanation has passed; the time for application has come.

At that point, it's appropriate for the preacher to leave behind "we" in favor of "you." No longer is the preacher representing the people to God; he is representing God to the people. "We've seen the biblical principle; we've seen two or three ways others have applied it. Now, what does this say to you?"

"You've got to decide how you're going to spend your money."

"You've got to decide whether you're going to take your marriage vows seriously."

It's you—not you plural, but you singular—you personally who must decide what you will do with the truth you've heard.

For the preacher to say "you" at that point isn't arrogant; he's not standing apart from the congregation. He's simply challenging each listener to make personal application.

In the final analysis, effective application does not rely on techniques. It is more a stance than a method. Life changing preaching does not talk to the people about the Bible. Instead, it talks to the people about themselves—their questions, hurts, fears, and struggles—from the Bible. When we approach the sermon with that philosophy, flint strikes steel. The flint of someone's problem strikes the steel of the Word of God, and a spark emerges that can set that person on fire for God.

 uestions to Consider

1. How does the preacher strike the right balance between biblical content and life application?

2. What is the distinction between exegesis and exposition?
3. What is the "So What?" of preaching?
4. What is the role of real-life examples in preaching?
5. How can you strike the balance between biblical content and life application in your sermon this week?

Bookshelf

Craddock, Fred B. *As One Without Authority: Essays on Inductive Preaching.* 1971. Nashville: Abingdon, 1979.

Dudiut, Michael, ed. *Handbook of Contemporary Preaching.* Nashville: Broadman, 1992.

Pitt-Watson, Ian. *A Primer for Preachers.* Grand Rapids: Baker, 1990.

Robinson, Haddon W. *Biblical Preaching.* Grand Rapids: Baker, 1980.

Robinson, Haddon W. *Biblical Sermons: How Twelve Preachers Apply the Principles of Biblical Preaching.* Grand Rapids: Baker, 1980.

Busting Out of Sermon Block

Preaching well is hard work. We're expected to be witty, warm, and wise. And then next week, we have to do it again. The great science fiction writer H. G. Wells reportedly said most people think only once or twice in a lifetime, whereas he had made an international reputation by thinking once or twice a year.

Lots of pastors have to think once (or more) a week! More often than we would like to admit, we begin preparing a sermon with the feeling not that we have something to say, but that we have to say something. Only one time in twenty do I start my preparation feeling that this sermon will go well. The creative process is accompanied with a feeling of ambiguity, uncertainty, of trying to make the unknown known.

Like the homemaker whose goal of three nutritious meals a day is complicated by toddlers making messes, demands of a part-time job, overflowing baskets of laundry, and a phone that won't stop ringing, the multiple demands of pastoral life make fresh thinking and sermon writing even more difficult.

People never die at convenient times. The administrative load preoccupies pastors with scores of details that won't go away. Emotional weariness from dealing with people problems drains creative energies. And speaking several times weekly outstrips your capacity to assimilate truth fully into your life.

Just as savvy homemakers find resourceful ways to feed their families—a deft combination of ten-minute recipes, healthy snacks, a microwave special, and a few full-course evening feasts—pastors, too, can find ways to keep tasty and balanced spiritual meals on the table.

Distinct Phases

When we feel we don't have anything to say in a sermon, it's usually because we've gotten ahead of ourselves. We're thinking about the sermon before we've understood the text. Instead, we need to divide our sermon preparation into two distinct phases.

1. What am I going to say? I start the process by focusing on content, not delivery. Approaching a text with the attitude 'How am I going to get a sermon out of this?' pollutes the process. We can end up manipulating the text for the purposes of an outline instead of first trying to observe, interpret, and appreciate the text.

For one message based on the story of Christ calming the storm, I began my study assuming my sermon's main idea would be that we can count on Christ to calm the wind and waves in our lives. But as I studied the text, I realized I couldn't promise people they would never sink just because Christ was with them in the storms of life.

This passage has to be seen in its broader context. Jesus has called the disciples and told them about the nature of his kingdom: it will start small but spread wide. In that early stage, everything depended on the men in that boat—Jesus and the disciples. If they go under, the kingdom is gone. The point of the passage is that those who have committed everything to Christ's cause can know that the kingdom will ultimately triumph because of the power of the King. This is an eternal truth that shifts the emphasis from the personal storms in my life and whether I will sink to the eternal kingdom that will never fail. If I promised that Christ would calm every storm, I would have twisted the text to say what I wanted. Instead I preached what the text taught me.

I have learned to let understanding the text dominate the sermon process early and later let sermonizing dominate. I have more material than I can preach when I first try to understand and interpret a text for its own sake. I ask, 'What is the biblical writer doing?' Then I study the context for the flow of thought. (I usually get more preachable insights from context than from studying the grammar and word structure of the original language.)

By studying the context, I came up with a major lead for a sermon on 1 Peter 5. "To the elders among you," writes Peter, "I appeal as a fellow elder, a witness of Christ's sufferings and one who also will share in the glory to be revealed" (v. 1). In my study, I found the theme of suffering accompanied by glory runs throughout 1 Peter. Whether in marriage, government, family—or church—when we suffer for Christ, we experience the glory of Christ. My sermon therefore pointed to this theme as it applied to leaders in the church.

2. How am I going to say it? In this phase I move to the communication question. How will I get the ideas I've uncovered in the passage across to people in a way that interests, informs, motivates, and changes them? Out of all that I could say about this passage, what will I choose to say?

This part of the process can also provide us with something significant to say. Early on I ask, Which of the following tacks is the biblical writer taking here: Is he primarily (a) explaining, (b) proving, or (c) applying?

If the passage majors in explanation, then my sermon will major in teaching. In the parable of the Pharisee and the tax collector (Luke 18:9–14), the primary purpose of this passage is to teach that the person who sees God as God and humbles himself before him is justified and exalted, and the person who exalts himself before God remains in his sins.

Accordingly, my sermon majors in explanation not exhortation. I dig beneath the assumptions we have about Pharisees and tax collectors, helping my listeners get into the minds of these two men. What did they think about themselves? What did others think about them? How would these roles look today? I talked about the nature of the sins of hypocrisy, self-righteousness, and disobedience.

One of the best ways to overcome "sermon block" is to think through the question, "What's hard to believe about this passage?"

We can underrate the need to prove the truth of a text. Even if there isn't a skeptical bone in our body, we need to ask, Will those who hear me believe this? Does this conform to my and their experience? If not, why not?

Our experience doesn't govern the Bible, but we need to explain perceived discrepancies between what the Bible says and our reality. Suppose someone hears the passage, "If two of you on earth agree on anything, it will be done for you." She wonders, "What if I want a blue Cadillac? If I can get two of the elders to agree with me in prayer, is that a done deal?" Like most people, she questions, "Do I believe that?"

In my sermon, I try to be an advocate for that person. She won't raise her hand and interrupt me, but like most people in the pews today, she listens to sermons with a keen sense of skepticism. The preacher who ignores that is ignoring reality. C. S. Lewis has been popular in recent decades largely because he deals with the "Is this really true?" question. He assumed people needed to be convinced.

Good ideas for preaching also emerge as we apply the Bible's truths to people's lives. Sermon ideas ignite when the flint of people's problems strikes the steel of God's Word.

Sometimes we can't come up with much to say because our thinking is too steely; it's all God's Word, but we don't link it to specific situations in contemporary life. Other times we come up short because we're too flinty; we're people-oriented, but we lack the authoritative content that only Scripture can bring.

But we almost always spark a preaching flame if we strike those two elements together. So part of my preparation is to ask these application questions: What difference does this make? What are the implications for our lives in this text? If someone takes this truth seriously and tries to live it on Monday morning, how will he or she live differently?

Kitchen Helpers

Like labor-saving devices in the kitchen, there are ways to write a sermon that can relieve the pressure of finding something to say. Here are six "kitchen helpers."

1. Develop a preaching calendar. Many pastors set up a plan for what they will preach over the next quarter, half-year, or year. We can take a retreat for several days and ask ourselves what the needs of the congregation are, what subjects we sense God impressing on our hearts, what themes we have an avid interest in.

A preaching calendar doesn't have to confine us. If some brilliant stroke from God strikes us, we can always change our preaching plans. But if not, when we walk into the study, we have a sense of well-thought-through, well-prayed-through direction. My calendars have been based primarily on expository series through complete books of the Bible (which provides more than enough grist for any mill).

Once a calendar is set, we can set up file folders for each series of sermons, which become repositories for the relevant material we come across in the weeks and months before the sermons are preached. When the time finally comes to begin preparing the sermon, we already have a file of illustrations, quotes, insights.

2. Work on sermons in ten-day cycles. The purpose of a longer cycle is to provide simmer time. On the Thursday ten days prior to the Sunday I will preach, I do my exegetical study. I read the text and think about it till I hit a wall. Then I write down what is holding me up: What words don't I understand? What issues can't I solve? What ideas don't make sense? If you can't state specifically where your problems are, you won't get answers.

Thus, ten days before I preach a sermon, I know what I need to be thinking about, which I do while driving the car, taking a shower, or laying awake at night. This also directs my reading. I know where the gaps in my understanding are, and I can more quickly find the answers. I can cull twenty commentaries in an hour if I know the key questions.

Often, when I sit down to resume study the following Tuesday, the issues in the passage are much clearer. I wonder, "What in the world was I so hung up about?"

When I preached a sermon on the seven churches of Revelation, I grew curious about the seven cities and how they affected the churches. I did some extra research that added significant insights. If I had been writing this sermon the day or two before preaching, I couldn't have done that.

My next study time in the cycle is five days later, on Tuesday, when I finish up my exegetical work and organize the sermon. By the end of Tuesday, I want at least to have the sermon's homiletical skeleton and introduction completed. I may also have begun shaping the main movements. My final writing installment takes place on Friday. I finish writing and actually have time to rearrange and polish.

3. Get double duty off study. Duane Litfin, president of Wheaton College, first introduced me to the idea of preparing two sermons from research on one preaching passage. When he was pastoring in Memphis, if his Sunday morning message primarily explained or proved the truth of a passage, on Sunday night he focused on application. Or, on Sunday night he developed a subtheme of a passage that couldn't be given justice in the Sunday morning message. In Philippians 2:1–11, for example, he might preach in the morning on Christlike humility and on Sunday night, the doctrine of Christ's humanity.

4. Think visually. Think of words on a spectrum, with abstract words and ideas at the top of the ladder and concrete ideas at the bottom. Scholars climb up the ladder of abstraction; communicators step down to get as close to specifics as possible.

When I have an idea without a specific picture in my mind, nothing interesting happens in me. But my mind starts to roll when I have an image.

When I study a text, I ask, "What image was in the biblical writer's mind as he wrote this?" If the subject is reconciliation, he didn't write about some abstract doctrine; he was thinking about enemies who made peace. As I study such a passage, I pose questions that keep me close to real life: "What's it like to have an enemy? Why is it so hard to make peace?" I'll think about countries in Europe, where people who have lived together for decades suddenly begin killing each other. "What happens when neighbors turn into enemies?"

I don't think about abstract ideas like "parenting." I think of bouncing a baby on my knee, of getting up in the middle of the night and staggering to a crib to a child who won't stop crying, and of the feelings of love and anger that go along with all this.

5. Work on a sermon out loud. My family learned that if they walk by my office and hear me mumbling, I'm working on a sermon. I get in imaginary conversations with people I want the sermon to help: "Robinson, you say God wants us to love our neighbors, but what do you do when you go to wash their feet and they kick you in the mouth? How many times do you get kicked before you say, 'Forget it'?"

"You have to get kicked three times," I'll continue out loud to myself, "and then you can break his toes. No, I wouldn't say that. What would I say?"

Working through a sermon aloud helps crystallize our thinking. It also gives us a feel for the flow of thought in the text.

6. Borrow. God doesn't give us any points for originality. He gives points for being faithful and clear. To have sitting on our shelves books from the great teachers of the world, people who have spent years of their lives studying a book like Romans, and not use them is to deny the many contributions of Christ's church. To think that in three hours of exegesis we're going to match the insights of those who've spent years studying a book is a mistake.

But save commentaries for later in the process. If we go to the commentaries too quickly, they frame our thoughts. But once I have read through a passage and know where my difficulties lie, commentators become my teachers.

Tributaries for High-Water Preaching

I have developed habits that help me collect material for sermons on an ongoing basis (not just for the sermon I will be preaching this Sunday). They are tributaries for high-water preaching.

First, I observe and interpret daily life. Helmut Thielicke said, "The world is God's picture book." We can waste a lot of experiences. There are lessons in every day's events, in things as mundane as getting stuck in traffic or hearing a joke.

This is especially so when something happens that touches us emotionally, either positively or negatively. Even if I don't immediately grasp its significance, I write the anecdote down on a 3 x 5 card and reflect on it. It's a piece of life that someday will fit some insight, illustration, or sermon.

Reading books and magazines and watching movies and television—even commercials—is another way of observing life.

I watched an Italian movie, *Jean de Florette*, which begins with a city dweller inheriting a farm, moving to the country, and trying to learn farming from books. Wanting the farm for themselves, some unscrupulous neighbors block a spring that irrigates the farm. The new owner, unaware that he owns spring water, prays for rain. Storm clouds gather, but the rain falls on the other side of the mountain, never watering his land. Eventually the man dies, and the corrupt men buy his farm for next to nothing. There the movie ends.

I turned off the VCR profoundly depressed. I said to my wife, "That's the way many people see the world. Evil triumphs— The End." If I ever preach on Ahab stealing Nabal's vineyard, though, that movie will be a part of my introduction.

The questions I ask about ads are, "What do they want people to do? And how are they motivating them?" Marketers spend millions of research dollars to learn what motivates people. Watching their ads, we see the results of their research.

In one recent ad, a school appealed for new students, stating repeatedly that their graduates make more money. The school didn't promise its classes would make students deeper, better people, or open the door to a more fulfilling career. The carrot being dangled was money. In preaching, I can use that ad to raise the question of whether money alone is ultimately going to satisfy.

As another tributary for high-water preaching, I make it a point to converse with people different from me.

I've learned to make the most of the power of questions: "How do you make your living? In your field of work, what are your biggest problems? Who are the successful people in your world? What makes people winners or losers to you? What do you have to worry about? If you could have anything in the world, what would it be?"

I once met a man who owned a plastics manufacturing company. "How do you compete with the big boys in your trade?" I asked.

"Service," he responded. "I give my customers the best service." He went on to describe the lengths he went to give his customers what they want. I realized that today, the product may not be as important to people as the attitude and service that come along with it. That may make it into a sermon on evangelism sometime.

One of the most meaningful conversations I've had recently was with a person who has AIDS. He had been involved in a homosexual relationship with a man with whom he thought he had a 'lovebonding relationship.' "He didn't tell me he had AIDS," he said sadly.

He described his fears of dying in a few years and his anger that someone he loved had done something that would kill him. He talked about his feelings of regret, of being ostracized, of wanting others to care but not sensing their care, of being sexually frustrated yet at the same time hating sex for its drawing power.

"I couldn't do to another human being what that man did to me," he said.

Through all of this, he had become a Christian. Talking with him helped me better understand people in such situations. Such conversations feed my soul and add richness to preaching.

Soul Attention

The more full our souls, the more we can preach without running dry.

Of the many spiritual disciplines that enlarge spirit, mind, and soul, we need to find the ones that benefit us the most.

I have a friend whose son has joined a monastery in pursuit of spirituality. He finds great benefit from the vow of silence and from long periods of meditation upon Scripture. Such disciplines have less benefit for me. But it is impossible for me to overstate how much my friendships with certain people have challenged me. Although being with large groups does more to drain me than stimulate me, I will rearrange my calendar just to spend a day or two with a friend.

We also need to recognize the difference between authentic growth and borrowed growth. I know a woman who has a tremendous appreciation for classical music. When she listens to a masterpiece, it is food for her soul. I envy her. I wish music stirred me as it does her. Sometimes when I hear her talk about music, I'm tempted to talk about music as she talks about music. But I would be impersonating a connoisseur.

In our early days as Christians and as preachers, we need mentors and models to get us started. The growth they inspire in us is authentic if their values truly become ours, not just something we value because so-and-so stresses it. But if we try to preach exactly as they do, the same life themes they had, we will lack integrity. If you keep doing it, eventually you're a counterfeit.

There's a difference between someone who derives great pleasure from meditating on a sunset and someone who meditates on sunsets because that's what "deep" people do. We can read in *Preachers and Preaching* what Martin Lloyd Jones says about the importance of urgency in preaching, but if we try to be more urgent without having the values and passions that produce urgency, our preaching will strike listeners as affected.

The ideas, themes, experiences, virtues, authors, and art that have gripped our souls are the ones that fill our preaching cup.

The number of issues that need to be addressed is so vast, the quantity of preaching material in Scripture so great, the needs of people so inexhaustible, a preacher couldn't finish the job in ten lifetimes. If we organize our sermonic work and stay full of God, more often than not, as we sit down to work out our sermons, we'll not only have something to say, we'll have more to say than time allows.

Questions to Consider

1. What does Haddon Robinson suggest as the approach to starting the process of sermon preparation?
2. What is the second phase of sermon preparation?
3. List some of the labor-saving devices.
4. What are some of the habits suggested for the collection of sermon material?
5. How can you cultivate your spiritual disciplines?

Bookshelf

Green, Michael P. *Green's Filing Systems*. Grand Rapids: Baker, 1991.

Hansen, David. *A Little Handbook on Having a Soul*. Downers Grove: InterVarsity, 1997.

Hostetler, Michael J. *Introducing the Sermon: The Art of Compelling Beginnings*. Grand Rapids: Zondervan, 1986.

Logan, Samuel T., Jr., ed. *The Preacher and Preaching: Reviving the Art in the Twentieth Century*. Phillipsburg, NJ: Presbyterian & Reformed, 1986.

Von Rad, Gerhard. *Biblical Interpretation in Preaching*. Translated by John Steely. Nashville: Abingdon, 1977.

The Preacher and People

NINE

Competing with the Communication Kings

Your sermon ends, and you're pleased with it. Then someone from the congregation approaches with a beaming smile.

"Nice sermon, Pastor. Say, did you hear Charles Stanley on television this morning? He has been preaching on grace for several weeks. Powerful messages! He says that . . ."

The church member means well, but you can't help but feel people are comparing you—unfavorably—with someone who is a ten-talent preacher, a communication king.

When I was in seminary, celebrated preachers spoke in our chapel and at local conferences: Harry Ironside, Vernon McGee, Roy Aldrich, Stephen Olford, Ray Stedman. After hearing these preachers, others were inspired. But I walked out of the service wanting to quit. I remember once reading a sermon by Peter Marshall and literally weeping in frustration because I could not produce a sermon approaching his. Reading a communication king made me want to get out of preaching altogether.

Many pastors can identify with those feelings. Today many more "kings" rule the homiletical landscape. Media preachers are some of the most gifted, and they enjoy extra advantages like researchers, audio or video engineers, and freedom from the drain of everyday pastoring.

In addition, local pastors preach in the communication age. Every day of the week, our people hear the best communication money can buy, from smooth TV news people, to dazzling entertainers, to hilarious comedians, all of whom are supplied with words by professional word smiths. Madison Avenue spends millions on thirty-second TV spots or one-page magazine ads that communicate with allure and power.

How have the communication kings affected the expectations people have for the preaching of the local pastor? In basketball, a dunk used to be a novelty, but now even the guards "play above the rim." Have the communication kings raised the level of play required of everyone? Does the local pastor have any advantages over communication kings? Are communication kings friends or competitors? What can we learn from them?

Jarred Judgment

We have to admit it: communication kings are skilled and talented. And they are good in the very field we've given our lives to. It's only natural for a pastor to feel intimidated.

We mustn't blow this out of proportion, however—which is precisely what preachers, given our make-up, are tempted to do. A pastor's soul is sensitive. All well and good, but the dark side is pastors tend to be more thin-skinned about slights and criticism. If twenty-five parishioners say, "Good sermon" to the pastor on their way out of church and one woman half-kiddingly says, "Well, there's always next week," we spend the rest of the afternoon wondering what she meant by that.

Two experiences of my own illustrate this hypersensitivity, which can cause us to doubt and sometimes misread the effect of our preaching.

Several years ago, I spoke at a youth workers convention, but I felt the message went poorly. When I used a key illustration out of place, it put me off balance. I had that sensation of mentally stepping outside myself and thinking about how badly my sermon was going even as I preached it. I noticed a few young people reading magazines.

When I finished, I felt the sermon had bombed, and I just wanted to escape the building.

Several months later, I was chatting with a couple of people who had been at the convention, who said, "We really appreciated your message." Assuming they were just being kind, I brushed off their comments.

Six months later still, I was packing for a trip and grabbed a handful of sermon tapes to listen to on the plane. The next day, as I rummaged through the tapes, I noticed that I had inadvertently grabbed the sermon from the youth convention, a message I had no intention of listening to again. But I changed my mind, and with a slight cringe, I put it in the tape player.

I was stunned. I had said what I had wanted to say in the sermon, and I felt I had said it well. Now that several months had passed, I could listen objectively. My feelings while preaching that sermon had not conformed to reality.

Of course, it works both ways. On another occasion, I spoke at a church and felt the sermon was a tremendous success. After the service, as I was waiting in the back of the sanctuary for the pastor, I noticed a pew card someone had written on. I read it with some dismay: "I wonder how long this guy's going to preach. There's going to be a long line at the cafeteria."

Obviously my sermon had not had much impact on this unknown scribbler.

The point is this: our high sensitivity to the effectiveness of our preaching sometimes jars our immediate judgment. And in relation to the communication kings, it puts us immediately on the defensive. When we recognize that, it already begins to relieve some of the pressure we feel. But there's more.

The Advantages of the Local Pastor

Although those who preach to national audiences via TV, radio, tapes, and conferences have a lot going for them, the local pastor also has some huge advantages. We're playing on a more level field than we imagine.

We benefit, first, from a personal, loving relationship with our listeners. When we stand in the pulpit, we have the credibility and spiritual authority that comes only from having been with people in their times of need. When we preach on the power of prayer, parishioners know us as the pastors who have interceded with them when they were unemployed. When we preach on compassion, they know us as preachers who have wept with them at the funeral home.

Our listeners know us, trust us, and see in us lives that largely back up what we preach. That example accomplishes more than mere homiletical skills ever can.

The local pastor also enjoys the advantage of local accent. Listeners quickly pick up when a speaker is an outsider.

I once heard a preacher use a baseball illustration by saying, "The batter got a four-base hit." People use the terms *two-base hit* and *three-base hit*, but anyone who knows baseball would say the batter hit a home run. The speaker, it turned out, was not American.

What's true on a national level is even more true at the local level. There are many local "accents" that only the local pastor can appreciate and use to advantage.

Language accents. In some parts of the country, people say supper for the evening meal; in others dinner is the word. Some towns use pop and others soda when referring to soft drinks. In New England we call milk shakes, freezes. Some regions speak more slowly, with a twang or drawl, others at a clipped rate. In the West, people say, I'm going with you." In the Midwest, they say, "I'm going with."

The preacher naturally adapts to such nuances, and thus identifies with people in a way national TV preachers cannot.

Social accents. In a blue-collar town, people tend to use rougher vernacular, and they usually disdain bookish language. They are suspicious of experts; instead, they respect common people and their common sense.

In a middle-class, college-educated suburb, people value higher education and use more abstract speech. They often defer to experts, and they respect sophistication.

The local pastor can tune his or her sermon to reflect these social accents. Furthermore, the local preacher can refer to town jokes or mention the nicknames for significant landmarks and buildings in the area.

For instance, in the Chicago area, "The El" is shorthand for one of the local commuter train systems, and "Metra" is the name for the other. By simply referring to one or the other in an illustration, the pastor will have set a scene that locals can identify with.

Historical accents. The local pastor knows the events significant to residents: the big fire, the great flood, the high school basketball championship year. A local pastor can say, "I read the obituary for Coach Peterson in the paper yesterday. You all knew him. He taught history to most of your children. He was a stalwart in our community, who inspired young people. He reminds us how vibrant and alive someone can be, and how quickly death comes."

A local illustration like that affects a congregation more profoundly than quoting Aristotle or Byron on death.

All these accents give the local pastor a rapport, a trust, the advantage of being an insider, someone who knows the people.

Thomas Long, former professor of preaching at Princeton Theological Seminary, once said that great preaching these days is local, that is, it arises out of and makes reference to local national following, but local preachers who can speak with the unique accents of their people can have a stronger impact.

Partners and Mentors

We do have advantages then. Still, the communication kings influence our congregations significantly, and we cannot pretend otherwise. We don't have to respond with insecurity and defensiveness though. Here are two positive responses that may help you take advantage of their ministries.

• *Be grateful.* It's natural to be jealous of the great preachers, though we rarely recognize jealousy as such. It usually takes the form of carping criticism of their ministries whenever their names are mentioned.

Communication kings attract jealousy like a picnic attracts ants. In a culture that honors individualism and competition, great communicators seem to have more "success" in ministry. And if someone else wins, we assume we have lost.

It doesn't have to be that way. A friend who pastors in Denver is learning to get over jealousy. Some time ago, a number of people left his church and started attending a nearby megachurch. He struggled with resentment and anger for several days. He decided his only hope was prayer, so he began praying for the megachurch and its pastor. He regularly prayed, "Thank you, God, that they are touching people we could never reach."

His attitude turned around. Thereafter, when he heard about successes of the megachurch, he could rejoice because his prayers were being answered. His praying helped him realize his church and the megachurch were on the same team, part of a larger network. When the bigger church succeeded, the team succeeded.

He's also learned to express that attitude from the pulpit. Publicly praying for "rival" preachers teaches a congregation and reinforces for the pastor the idea that small ministries aren't competing with large.

In a similar way, if a parishioner says, "I really get a lot out of Charles Stanley's sermons. You ought to watch him," we can respond, 'Isn't it wonderful the way God has given these gifts to Charles Stanley and how he's reaching so many people?" It sounds corny, but it's an old idea, and a biblical idea, and I've discovered it works. We can rejoice with those who rejoice.

The highest goal of team members is to win. The woman who swims the second lap in the relay is grateful that her teammate took the final lap in record time. Rivalry—and thus jealousy—isn't the issue. The gold medal is, and so gratefulness is her usual attitude.

• *Imitate strengths—not weaknesses.* The Michael Jordan's of the preaching world inspire us to, as the commercial says, "be like Mike." Easier said than done. Ironically, what pastors often imitate are the communication kings' idiosyncrasies and weaknesses.

Communication kings succeed despite their weaknesses, not because of them. But their idiosyncrasies are so visible, that's what those who imitate them pick up on.

One prominent preacher had the habit of gesturing a phrase too late. He'd say, "It was a wide, wide desert," and then a half-second later, he'd spread his arms wide. With him it never distracted; his strengths overcame his problem. Dozens of his followers, however, now gesture late, and it looks like a cheap imitation.

Another celebrated preacher shakes his leg whenever he gets wired up. For him, that's an endearing mannerism. But when those trained by him do the same thing it looks as though they have a nerve disease.

Some successful preachers of the past loudly sucked air or said, "Amen," between virtually every sentence. Many have imitated them, to their detriment.

In order to learn from the strengths of great preachers, we need to listen to one of their sermons three or four times. It takes that many hearings to get some emotional distance from the sermon and analyze what the speaker is doing.

First, try to understand what the sermon does well and then ask why. Does it affect your emotions in an authentic way? Compel your interest in the introduction? End with a great sense of resolution and inspiration? Why are the main points so memorable? What gave the sermon authority?

In addition to analyzing sermons, we can profit from the continuing study of homiletics, which provides us with the categories we need in order to analyze what effective communicators do.

For example, my continuing study of preaching books and articles has helped me see how modern listeners have evolved. Modern listeners respond well to an inductive approach to sermons, where a number of examples from life are given and then principles extracted from them. Listeners are a bit bored when we begin by expounding principles, even if the principles are illustrated. Many modern hearers prefer to explore a subject and discover answers along with the preacher, rather than simply being told the conclusions.

Once I became aware of this pattern in modern communication, I was able to notice how effective communicators exploited it successfully.

Every year I choose a different noted preacher, some living and others from the past—Peter Marshall, Charles Finney, Alexander Maclaren—and study him for a full year. I read his sermons and his biography. If possible, I listen to or view tapes of his sermons. I read anything I can find about how he prepared sermons. Then when I get stumped in the middle of writing a sermon, I can ask myself, "How would Spurgeon have handled this? What would Clovis Chappell do to make this live?"

I also study secular communication kings to figure out their approaches. I was watching John Bradshaw, a pop psychologist who talks about relationships and the inner child. I concluded that part of Bradshaw's popularity stems from his talking to people about people. I wondered, Does simply applying the Bible to people make people feel preached at? Does talking about their lives from the Bible, using the Scriptures as a way to explain their experiences, their struggles, and then bringing in the Bible's solutions help them listen? That's a subtle difference that may have a major effect on how secular listeners respond.

One characteristic of great athletes is they can make everyone around them play better. They aren't just stars; they make ordinary players into a star team.

The communication kings may have made me feel insecure and at times inadequate, but I'm a better preacher today because of them. Their examples have inspired, challenged, and instructed me. We may not all play above the rim, but they've elevated our games, helping each of us to make the most of the one, two, or ten "talents" God has given us. We're not competing against the communication kings; we're competing with them.

uestions to Consider

1. What jars our judgment in assessing our sermons? Why?
2. What are the advantages of being a local pastor?
3. What are the positive responses Robinson suggests for preachers to take advantage of their ministries?
4. What are the challenges you face as you deal with the communication kings?
5. What can you do to improve your ability to communicate?

ookshelf

Hansen, David. *The Power of Loving Your Church: Leading Through Acceptance and Grace.* Minneapolis: Bethany House, 1998.

Jacks, G. Robert. *Just Say the Word: Writing for the Ear.* Grand Rapids: Eerdmans, 1996.

Lowry, Eugene L. *The Homiletical Plot.* Atlanta: John Knox, 1980.

Radecke, Mark William. *In Many and Various Ways: Exploration in Sermonic Form.* Lima, OH: C.S.S., 1985.

Reierson, Gary B. *The Art in Preaching: The Intersection of Theology, Worship, and Preaching with the Arts.* Lanham, MD: University Press of America, 1988.

TEN

Preaching to Everyone in Particular

HOW TO SCRATCH WHERE PEOPLE NICHE

While Grace Chapel in Lexington, Massachusetts, was without a pastor for over a year, I preached there often. The church is remarkably diverse, having Harvard professors and high school dropouts, doctors and lawyers and house cleaners, political activists and those who don't even read the newspaper, people with multimillion-dollar investment portfolios and minimum-wage workers. In addition, members are of many races and colors.

I stood before such diversity each week amazed at the responsibility I had to reach them all. As I prepared my sermons, I stewed over how my sermon could reach the entire cross-section.

As preachers, our task can be expressed simply: to become all things to all people. To actually do it is a formidable task.

Sacrificing What Comes Naturally

When we fail to speak to the entire cross-section in our churches, we resemble the doctor who knows only how to set

118

a broken arm: if a patient complains of a bellyache, the doctor breaks his arm so she can set it.

Reaching broader audiences demands that we sacrifice what comes naturally to us. When Paul said, "I have become all things to all men so that by all possible means I might save some" (1 Cor. 9:22), he wasn't talking about just evangelism. He was talking also about helping converts grow. "To the weak"—believers who had weak consciences—he became weak; he restricted his freedom for their sake.

Speaking to a broader audience requires a sacrifice from us. We give up our freedom to use certain kinds of humor, to call minority groups by names that make sense to us, to illustrate only from books and movies we find interesting, to speak only to people with our education and level of Christian commitment. Sometimes such sacrifice feels constricting to us.

A pastor who objects strongly to the women's movement, for example, might take a passing shot at its leaders and activities. By doing so, though, he risks needlessly alienating women in the congregation.

Sacrificing what comes most naturally to us, though, is what gives us a platform from which to speak. Just as a legalistic Jew wouldn't regard Paul as credible if Paul ignored the law, so many women, for example, won't regard a preacher as credible if he shows zero sensitivity to their issues.

Why go to all this trouble? Because it is right and because it is wise.

The people we are most likely to offend are those on the edge, those cautiously considering the gospel or deeper commitment but who are skittish, easily chased away by one offensive move from pastors. Those already secure in the fold will probably stick by us in spite of our blunders. The new people we're trying to reach are as easily spooked as wild turkeys.

A young couple moved into a Chicago suburb and attended one church for several months. The church helped them through the husband's unemployment. Several times the pastor met with the man, who had advanced degrees in ecology and was interested in deeper involvement in the church.

Then he and his wife abruptly stopped coming. The pastor repeatedly tried to contact them, and finally after several months, he was able to take the man out for lunch. He asked him why they had not come to church in such a long time.

"In several of your sermons," the man replied, "you made comments that belittled science. If that is the way you feel, I don't think we're on the same wavelength."

The pastor remembered the remarks, which were either passing comments or rhetorical flourishes contrasting the power of Christ and the weakness of human thought. But the consequence was not passing: a man who showed promise of moving into deeper discipleship had been diverted.

How can we gain appreciation for lives unlike our own, for people as different as security guards and investment bankers?

The same way novelists do: listening and observing. Listen to the people you counsel and the conversations around you in restaurants and stores. Observe characters in movies and common people interviewed on the news. Note how these people state their concerns, their specific phrasing, their feelings, their issues. Get an ear for dialog.

I know one pastor who holds a focus group each Thursday before he preaches. He eats lunch with several people from diverse backgrounds, tells them the ideas in his sermon, and asks them how they hear these ideas. They often raise issues that had never occurred to him.

After one service a woman told me how she and several other African-Americans had taken out an ad in the *New York Times* to explain their resentment of homosexual activists who draw on the black experience to describe their own. "They identified themselves as a minority," she told me. "We're both minorities, but that's the only thing we have in common. They don't know what we've gone through. They don't know the pain of being black."

She helped me understand what a disadvantaged minority feels, and someday I'm sure I'll include in a sermon how God can help those who feel the pain of being black in America.

Targeting Particular Audiences

In the Gospels we see that Christ never dealt with two people the same way. He told the curious Pharisee that he needed to be born again, the woman at the well that she needed living water. He brought good news to each individual, but at the person's point of contact.

The New Testament epistles differ from each other because they brought the same basic theology to bear on diverse problems. In 1 Corinthians, Paul defended the doctrine of the Resurrection against those who doubted it; in 1 Thessalonians, Paul brought that same truth to believers who were worried about those who had already died in Christ. From the Bible's beginning to its end, we see God adjusting the message to the audience without sacrificing the truth. Truth is never more powerfully experienced than when it speaks to someone's personal situation.

Knowing that, some preachers try not to exclude listeners and fall into preaching in generalities. For example, if I say, "Irritation bothers us all," I'm speaking to no one in particular. A sermon full of generalities hits no one in particular.

We do better to focus specifically on two or three types of people in a message (changing who those two or three groups are each week). The surprising thing is that the more directed and personal a message, the more universal it becomes.

I might illustrate a sermon on conflict by saying, "You live with your roommate, and your roommate has some irritating habits, like not cleaning the dishes right after the meal. Or you're married, and your husband comes home and plops himself in front of the TV without any regard for what your day has been like." Although these two scenarios don't fit all listeners, all can identify with these specific experiences and the feelings they elicit.

To help me speak to what different members of an audience may be going through, I use a suggestion given by a good friend, Don Sunukjian. I prepare my sermons using a life situation grid.

Across the top of the grid, I label columns for men, women, singles, married, divorced, those living together. On the side of the grid, I have rows for different age groups (youth, young adult, middle-age, elderly), professional groups (the unemployed, the self-employed, workers, and management), levels of faith (committed Christians, doubters, cynics, and atheists), the sick and the healthy, to name a few. I develop my grid based on the congregation and community I am preaching to.

After I've researched my biblical text and developed my ideas, I wander around the grid, looking for two to four intersections where the message will be especially relevant.

For instance, in one sermon on money, based on the Parable of the Shrewd Branch Manager in Luke 16, I went through my grid and thought of a widow in the congregation whose late husband, the president of a major corporation, had left her a large amount of money. She once had said to me, "What a curse it is to have a lot of money and take God seriously." Since I knew others in the congregation had significant incomes, I thought specifically about how someone with money would hear and feel about this passage.

A second intersection on the grid I explored was the working poor. For their sake, in the sermon I mentioned that Christ focuses on the attitude of our hearts, not on the amount we give.

A third group of special concern were visitors who might say afterward, "All pastors do is preach about money." Seeing them on the grid caused me to include some humor and speak directly to the objection.

On occasion, I can even preach an entire sermon to one particular group in the church—say, young men or women in business, or teenagers. I might introduce it by saying, "This morning I want to talk only to the teenagers. Some of you adults enjoy a short winter's nap on Sunday morning anyway, but this morning I give you permission to do so. Today I want to talk to young people in junior and senior high. You are an important part of this church, and I'd appreciate it if you would listen." All the application in that sermon would be for young people, but only a rare adult would tune out. In fact, information overheard can be more influential than information received directly.

Illustrating Broadly

Though we preach each week to diverse congregations and need to target particular subgroups, all listeners have these desires:

- They want to meet God or run away from him.
- They want to learn something.
- They want to laugh.
- They want to feel significant.
- They want to be motivated, in a positive way, to do better.
- They want a pastor to understand their pain and the difficulty they have doing what's right, without letting them off the hook.

One of the most important tools for addressing these universal concerns is through illustrations. People identify with people more than ideas. They gossip about people, not principles. Good stories transcend individual experiences so that people from a variety of situations can gain something from them. When hearing a story, listeners tell the story to themselves, inserting their own experiences and images.

An older woman once said to me, "Sometimes the Christian life is like washing sheets." She described how she washed sheets by hand in a large washing bucket, and when she would push one part of the sheet under water, air bubbles would move to another part of the sheet and float that section above water.

"I push it down here, it comes up there," she said. "I can never keep the whole sheet under water."

As she described the scene, her story became my story. My mind jumped back a half century to my boyhood. I recalled my mother's washing clothes in a tub and having the same problem.

To help listeners make emotional connections to my preaching, I try to illustrate broadly. I am tempted to draw many of my illustrations from sports, which may or may not appeal to the majority of women (more than half of most congregations). I intentionally try to include illustrations that more women may identify with, stories focused on relationships, drawn from the worlds of home and family or what they experience in the workplace.

As I watch TV I look for illustrations. My own tendency is to draw from what I read, but most people in a congregation do not read the materials I read. They live in a different sphere from mine, and I try to honor that in my sermons.

The essential thing about the stories I choose to tell is that all listeners be able to put themselves into the scene, becoming participants in the story.

I heard Gordon MacDonald do this masterfully while preaching about John the Baptist. Gordon presented an imaginative updating of John's ministry in a story that every listener could enter. It went something like this:

Several management types were at the River Jordan as the crowds came to John, and they decided they needed to get things organized. So they set up tables and begin to give tags to those coming for repentance.

On the tag is written the person's name and chief sin.

Bob walks up to the table. The organizers write his name on the tag and then ask, "What's your most awful sin, Bob?"

"I stole some money from my boss."

The person at the table takes a marker and writes in bold letters EMBEZZLER and slaps it on Bob's chest.

The next person comes forward. "Name?"

"Mary."

"Mary, what's your most awful sin?"

"I gossiped about some people. It wasn't very much, but I didn't like those people."

The organizers write, MARY—SLANDERER, and slap it on her.

A man walks up to the table. "Name?"

"George."

"George, what's your most awful sin?"

"I've thought about how nice it would be to have my neighbor's Corvette."

GEORGE—COVETER.

Another man approaches the table. "What's your name?" he is asked.

"Gordon."

"What's your sin?"

"I've had an affair."

The organizer writes GORDON—ADULTERER and slaps the sticker on his chest.

Soon Christ comes to be baptized. He walks down the line of those waiting to be baptized and asks them for their sin tags. One by one, he takes those tags off the people and sticks them on his own body. He goes to John, and as he is baptized, the river washes away the ink from each name tag he bears.

As Gordon told that story, everyone in the congregation mentally wrote his own sin and slapped it on his own chest. The illustration was specific but touched on universal feelings.

To come up with images and stories that nearly everyone can own, I sometimes write "idea networks" on a sheet of paper. If I'm talking about home, for example, I'll write the word *home* in the center of a sheet of paper, circle the word, and then surround it with any associations that come to my mind: "home sweet home," "welcome home," "it's good to have you home again," "home on the range," "going home for Christmas," "stole home."

These associations will inspire other associations and memories, some personal, some cultural. What I'm doing is digging into the phrases and images our culture associates with home. Somewhere from that page I'll come up with one or more images or stories with larger appeal.

Taking Listeners' Side

I do everything I can to show people I respect them and I'm on their side. It's another way I try to be all things to all people.

For instance, in my preaching I cultivate a conversational tone. Many people in our culture resent an authoritarian, lecturing manner. That style is what moderns mean when they use preaching in a pejorative sense ("Don't preach at me!"). They consider it patronizing and narrow-minded.

I also try to show empathy. When I quote from Malachi, "God hates divorce," I know there are divorced people sitting in the congregation who may begin to feel that God and Haddon Robinson hate them. So I'll follow up that verse with, "Those of you who are divorced know that better than anyone. You understand why God hates divorce. Not because he hates divorced people but because of what divorce does to people. You have the scars. Your children have the scars. You can testify to what it does. God hates divorce because he loves you."

I've found if listeners know you love and identify with them, they will let you say strong things. Most people are just asking that you be aware of them and not write them off.

Another way I tell listeners I'm on their side is by being careful with terms. Even though you're sure you don't have a bias, a listener may think you do if your phrasing offends them.

I try to use gender-inclusive language. If I'm telling a story about a doctor, I might say, "A surgeon stands in the operating room. As she takes the scalpel in her hand. . . ." I intentionally use *she* over *he* in strategic spots.

I also employ terms like spokesperson instead of spokesman. I say "he or she" instead of always saying "he"; or I use "he" sometimes and "she" other times. Even a few female pronouns in a sermon make a difference. (Here's a radical experiment: try using she all through a sermon except when you must use the masculine pronoun. You will get a sense of how much of preaching has a male flavor.)

I call minority groups what they want to be called. This is simple courtesy: If someone's name is Charles, and he doesn't like being called Charlie or Chuck, I'm obligated to call him Charles. I used to say Negroes, then Blacks. I used the term Afro-American in a recent sermon, and afterward a woman kindly corrected me, "It's African-American."

Not Compromising the Truth

Of course, no matter how hard we try, we're still going to offend people. Sometimes we need to apologize from the pulpit. "In last week's sermon, my humor was in bad taste. I described overweight people with a term that was hurtful. I'm sorry. I sometimes say things I don't mean, and you're gracious enough to tell me about it. Bear with me."

While preaching at Grace Chapel, I received at least a letter a week reacting to my sermons. When someone writes me, I always write back. Some people send thoughtful letters, and I owe them a thoughtful response. Sometimes they're dead right; they catch me in a prejudice. I have to admit that.

Sometimes you get letters in which people are vitriolic through no fault of yours. The best you can do is say, "Thank you for writing. I'm sorry I offended you. I wanted to communicate a great truth of Scripture and failed to get that across to you. I'm sorry."

But if we focus too hard on not offending, or if we read too many letters from the offended, we can become paralyzed. We start qualifying every sentence. We end up with weasel sermons that are defensive, cautious, and spineless.

Yes, at Christmas we need to acknowledge that for some people it's the most depressing time of the year, but we can't let that rob the season's joy from the congregation. Yes, on Mother's Day childless women feel extra pain, and we can acknowledge that, but everyone has a mother to honor, and we shouldn't squelch the church's honoring of them.

Although I'm aware of the land mines, I try not to get uptight, defensive, or hostile in the pulpit, for that only provokes people to be more easily offended. Saying, "You shouldn't be so sensitive," or "I get so sick of all this politically correct language," does no one—you or your people—any good.

And there are times when a pastor must preach truth at the expense of some sensitivities, yet we must do so with a burden in our hearts, not chips on our shoulders. There is no greater courage required of pastors than to preach what may cost them their pulpits.

There will always be a healthy discomfort as we try to be all things to all people. It's biblical, but it demands we walk a fine line. We want to be as appealing as possible but not at the cost of compromising the message. When we walk that line well, though, we experience something unequaled: a variety of people with a variety of concerns from a variety of settings all attentively listening to the good news.

 uestions to Consider

1. What does it mean to sacrifice what comes most naturally when preaching?
2. How does one target particular audiences?
3. What role does illustrations play in reaching one's listeners?
4. How can one take the listener's side when preparing to preach?
5. How are you going to scratch your listeners' niche in your next sermon?

ookshelf

Berkley, James D., ed. *Preaching to Convince.* Leadership Library Volume B. Dallas: Word, 1986.

Chapell, Bryan. *Using Illustrations to Preach with Power.* Grand Rapids: Zondervan, 1992.

Flynn, Leslie B. *Come Alive with Illustrations: How to Find, Use, and File Good Stories for Sermons and Speeches.* Grand Rapids: Baker, 1987.

Miller, Calvin. *Spirit, Word, and Story: A Philosophy of Marketplace Preaching.* Grand Rapids: Baker, 1996.

Read, David H. C. *Preaching About the Needs of Real People.* Philadelphia: Westminster, 1988.

ELEVEN

Listening to the Listeners

"What do you think of sermons?" the Institute for Advanced Pastoral Studies asked churchgoers—and got an earful. Sample responses:

"Too much analysis and too little answer."

"Too impersonal, too propositional—they relate nothing to life."

"Most sermons resemble hovercrafts skimming over the water on blasts of hot air, never landing anyplace!"

No wonder sermons are occasionally mocked as "the fine art of talking in someone else's sleep." Communication experts dismiss them as "religious monologues." Communication flows best on two-way streets, they argue, while preaching moves in only one direction. And because congregations can't talk back to register doubts, disagreements, or opinions, many sermons hit dead ends.

A second rap is that most ministers overcommunicate. They load new concepts and duties on the congregation before previous ideas can be digested and absorbed. Content keeps coming, but when frustrated listeners can't stop the conveyor belt, they stop listening.

Yet monologues afflict the clergy like a genetic disease. Experiments with dialogue sermons, in vogue a few years ago, have gone the way of the CB radio. What is more, those trained in theological seminaries, where content is king, succumb to the empty-jug fallacy. Getting ideas into someone else's head is akin to filling a jug with water. Preachers invest large segments of time gathering water from books, commentaries, and old class notes but seldom consider time spent with people a valuable resource. While they often possess the gift, knowledge, and fiery enthusiasm, their sermons sound like "manualese"—textbook exegesis. The empty-jug fallacy is summed up in a bit of doggerel:

> Cram it in, jam it in;
> People's heads are hollow.
> Take it in, pour it in;
> There is more to follow.

Heads are neither open nor hollow. Heads have lids, screwed on tightly, and no amount of pouring can force ideas inside. Minds open only when their owners sense a need to open them. Even then, ideas must still filter through layers of experience, habit, prejudice, fear, and suspicion. If ideas make it through at all, it's because feedback operates between speaker and listener.

In recent years, auto makers have begun outfitting some models with fuel efficiency gauges to let drivers know how their habits affect consumption. Whenever you stomp on the accelerator, the needle plummets; whenever you drive gently, the indicator rises. Very quickly this feedback helps pinpoint wasteful actions.

Preaching seems to be a zero-feedback situation, a monologue with no return. It does not have to be so. The pull toward monologue can be broken. In fact, significant preaching has always involved dialogue. The most astute preachers allow their eyes and ears to program their mouths. As they stand in the pulpit, they respond to cues from the audience telling them how they are doing. As they prepare, they study not only content but also people, hearing the spoken and unspoken questions. After speaking, they listen intently to find out how they have done.

Importance of Feedback

Most people do not realize that important feedback takes place during the act of preaching. Listening seems passive—a typical Sunday spectator sport. Yet able communicators listen with their eyes. They know that audiences show by their expressions and posture when they understand, approve, question, or are confused. People nod agreement, smile, check their watches, or slump in their seats. Great preachers do not build strong churches nearly as often as great churches through their feedback make strong preachers. These congregations give their preachers the home court advantage by actively listening to what they have to say.

Feedback, however, begins as the sermon is still brewing. Here pastors hold an advantage over other speakers, since they interact daily with members of the audience. Yet this advantage is not automatic. To benefit, preachers must listen: to questions people ask, and for answers they seek. They must observe: needs (expressed or unexpressed, admitted or denied), relationships (personal, family, community), experiences, attitudes, and interests. Jotting down what they observe each day will help take note of the passing parade. This in turn colors and shapes the handling of biblical material and the approach to the message. Let a preacher take a truth from Scripture and force himself to find twenty-five illustrations of that truth in daily life, and he will discover how much the world and its citizens have to tell him.

This dialogue with the congregation and the wider community can be more focused. In order to develop a sensitivity to current questions, John Stott, the internationally known English minister, joined a reading group that met monthly. They explored the ideas and implications of significant books, usually secular, from a Christian perspective. At times they attended films or plays together and then returned to the church to discuss what they had seen.

When Stott preached on contemporary issues, he formed an ad hoc group of specialists to help him learn the personal dimensions of the problem. At some of these gatherings, Stott actively participated, while at others he merely sat and eavesdropped on discussions between different points of thought. As an outgrowth of the challenging dialogue, Stott's sermons, while solidly biblical, were as up-to-date as next week's news magazine.

Pastors in smaller churches legitimately object that such groups develop more easily in large urban or suburban congregations. Yet even in rural and inner city communities, men and women wrestle with substantive issues, and many would welcome the opportunity to discuss contemporary life and thought with a minister.

Churches, large or small, can organize systems of feedback. A church in Iowa turns monologue to dialogue by basing its midweek Bible study on the passage for the following Sunday's sermon. The pastor provides notes explaining the text, and then the people divide into small groups to explore further meanings and implications for themselves. Out of this encounter, the pastor zeroes in on terms, ideas, and issues he must address and, as an added benefit, often finds illustrations and applications for his sermon. Surprisingly, everyone agrees studying the passage beforehand heightens rather than diminishes interest in the sermon. They are made aware of the biblical material, and they become curious about how the preacher will handle it.

A pastor of a small church in Oregon goes over his sermon with members of his board every Thursday at breakfast. Everyone reads the passage beforehand, and the minister takes a few moments to sketch the broad outline of his message. During the discussion that follows, each shares what the passage says and what it might mean to the congregation. While the minister prepares the sermon, he does not do so in solitary confinement; instead he benefits from the insights and experiences of others in the body of Christ.

Practicing Your Preaching

Rehearsing the sermon aloud also offers opportunity for feedback. John Wesley read some of his sermons to an uneducated servant girl with the instruction, "If I use a word or phrase you do not understand, you are to stop me." By this exercise, the learned Methodist developed the language of the mines and marketplace. Many preachers have taken a lead from Wesley. Some have risked their marriages by practicing on their wives. Since preachers' wives marry "for better or for worse," they can cut their down side risks by offering constructive criticism. When I was at Denver Seminary courses were offered to equip spouses in making their spouses' sermons better. Less courageous ministers—or those with weaker marriages—might run through their sermons with a shut-in or a friend willing to contribute an ear.

As people file out of the sanctuary on Sunday, they mumble appropriate clichés: "You preached a good sermon today" or "I enjoyed what you had to say." While these responses are nice, they are often little more than code words to get past the minister as he guards the door. Preachers need an organized program of feedback following the sermon to determine whether they have hit their target.

Oak Cliff Bible Fellowship in Dallas, Texas, devotes the last fifteen minutes of the service to questions and answers. Some sermons raise more questions than others, of course. When questions are few, members tell what the sermon could mean in their lives. Both questions and testimony not only benefit the people but provide immediate information to the pastor.

According to Reuel Howe, feedback sessions are more productive if the minister is not present. In his book *Partners in Preaching*, Howe suggests inviting six or more lay people, including a couple of teenagers, to take part in a reaction group following the church service. The pastor does not attend, but the conversation is recorded. When the tape runs out, the session ends. The pastor listens to the recorded comments later in the week. Several questions structure interaction.

1. What did the sermon say to you?
2. What difference, if any, do you think the sermon will make in your life?

3. How did the preacher's method, language, illustrations, and delivery help or hinder your hearing of the message?
4. Do you disagree with any of it? What would you have said about the subject?

Lay people find these opportunities stimulating. In fact, through them, many learn to listen to sermons more perceptively and develop a keener appreciation for good preaching. If the minister listens carefully, he will discover how his congregation responded, what they heard and did not hear, what they understood and did not understand.

However it comes about, feedback is the lifeblood of communication. Without it, preaching seldom touches life.

When the church was young, Christians gathered at a common meal for Communion and communication. As a teacher explained the Scriptures, listeners broke in with questions and comments. So lively was the feedback that New Testament writers like Paul wrote ground rules to keep this interchange under control. Later, as Christianity fell under the influence of Greek and Roman rhetoric, oratory replaced conversation, and dialogues became monologues.

The infant church possessed what the modern church must rediscover. Only as we talk with people—not at them—will preaching remain a vital and effective carrier of God's truth.

> Nothing could more surely convince me
>   of God's unending mercy
> than the continued existence on earth
>   of the church.
>
>   Annie Dillard

Questions to Consider

1. What is the role of feedback?
2. What can you do to become a better listener of your congregation?

3. What questions (of your listeners) can you ask while you are preparing your sermon?

4. What can good listening do for the preacher?

 ookshelf

Craddock, Fred B. *Preaching*. Nashville: Abingdon, 1985.

Farra, Harry. *The Sermon Doctor: Prescriptions for Successful Preaching*. Grand Rapids: Baker, 1989.

Galli, Mark, and Craig Brian Larson. *Preaching that Connects*. Grand Rapids: Zondervan, 1994.

Howe, Reuel. *Partners in Preaching: Clergy and Laity in Dialogue*. New York: Seabury, 1967.

Loscalzo, Craig A. *Preaching Sermons that Connect: Effective Communication Through Identification*. Downers Grove: IVP, 1992.

Preaching Sense about Dollars

A Madison Avenue advertising firm surveyed nonchurched people a few years ago and asked them their impressions of church. "The problem with church," respondents said, "is that the people are always sad, or they talk about death, or they ask for money."

In response to these prevailing attitudes, many churches today are upbeat, don't say much about death, and rarely broach the offensive subject of money.

Of course, a desire for evangelistic effectiveness is not the only reason we preachers are reluctant to talk about money. Many people, both inside the church and out, feel money is filthy lucre. One layman boasted to me that in the ten years his pastor had been there, the pastor had never once preached on money, but the church had done well financially. The thinking seems to be, *If we can get by without talking about money, all the better.*

Finally, there's our ever-present nervousness that listeners will perceive we are benefiting personally, that we have a vested interest in speaking on the topic.

The result, in my perception, is that today's growing-up generation has not been challenged about giving. Statistics reveal that people under forty contribute only about two percent of their income to charitable causes. If you were to ask people over fifty who have grown up in the church, "What should a Christian give?" they'd say, "A tithe." I don't think you'd get that response from the younger generation. Whether or not they agree with tithing, they have not been taught to give. Giving in church, for many of them, is seen as paying admission: *You pay $15 to go to a hockey game and $6 for a movie, so this service is worth about $10 to me.* Because it's unpopular, the idea that giving is a theological matter and a major expression of your Christian faith has been, for the most part, lost.

How do we begin to recover the ministry of giving for our congregations? How can we talk about money in a wholly faithful yet winsome way? Over the years I've wrestled with those questions. Here are some of the things I've learned about how to—and how not to—bring up the subject of money.

Subtle Temptations

First, I realize that I face subtle temptations whenever I prepare a message on giving. Here are four snares I try to avoid.

• *To unwittingly use guilt to motivate.* The New Testament's motivation for giving is grace; giving is an act of worship in response to the generosity of God to us. You are to give, Paul says, "as God has prospered you." If we really understand what God has given us, there will be a red streak of blood in our giving.

But often in preaching, we pound home a strong sense of *ought*: "Because of what God has given, you *ought* to give more. You *ought* to give ten percent." Or we foster guilt through comparisons: "Look at the house you live in; look at the car you drive; look at the clothes you wear. And then look at all of the need in the world, the hungry people and destitute." Those contrasts are enormous, but if we're not careful, such comparisons create only a feeling of guilt rather than gratitude. And gratitude is the healthy, biblical impetus for giving.

• *To not clearly define the scriptural promise that givers will receive.* Second Corinthians 8 and 9 teaches clearly, in the context of discussing money, that "he who sows bountifully will also reap bountifully." God blesses those who give with generosity. Personally, if my wife, Bonnie, and I were listing empirical evidences for the Christian faith, one would be the resurrection of Christ, but another would be in this area of giving. We have been astonished that again and again when we have given—with pain—God has supplied money for us from an unexpected source later.

But we must beware of using that as motivation. We dare not turn giving into a business deal with God. To give ten percent in order to get back twenty percent runs contrary to the whole ethic of the gospel. Anybody who's got a lick of sense would be glad to double her money, but the spiritual principle doesn't work that way. It's not tit for tat, one for one. In society, you give to an art museum so you can have your name on the new wing, but in God's family, you give to please your Father in heaven. The question is not "What do I get out of it?" but "What does God get out of it?"

• *To overemphasize the truth that everything belongs to God.* It's true that everything I have belongs to God. The Bible teaches that. But if I'm not careful, I can produce from that theological statement the implication that a person, if he's wholly committed, will put his entire paycheck in the offering plate. I don't know anyone who on a consistent basis can give everything he or she has to God without starving to death. It becomes an impossible ethic; the bar is always at eighteen feet, and I can jump only nine. When we preach the impossible dream, people don't take it seriously.

• *To teach on money primarily when it's needed.* I know of a church that, in order to erect some buildings, went out on a four-million-dollar limb. The leaders have committed the church to the entire amount and borrowed the money from the banks. They are still three million dollars short. That shortage stares the pastor in the face every month, so he's constantly on his people about money. His preaching insinuates, "If you folks were giving as God wants you to give, we would have no problem." This kind of scolding, for the person in the pew, is like meeting a bill collector at church every Sunday. Ultimately such preaching on money becomes counterproductive.

While that may be an extreme case, the principle holds true. When you're trying to raise money, and you continually preach on money because you need it, people sense your desperation. As a seminary president, I understood well the importance of asking for money, but teaching on money only when it's needed too easily begins to pressure rather than instruct. I accomplish more when someone can hear the sermon and say, "He talked about my money, but he wasn't begging for my money for his emergency."

Connect with People's Needs

Fortunately, we can sidestep these temptations and step forward with confidence, provided we follow a few key principles.

The first borrows a fundamental idea from communication: identify a need in the audience and speak to it. Most preachers do this every Sunday, connecting the timeless truths of the Bible with contemporary needs. But when it's time to preach on money, too often we think, *What do people really want to hear about money? They don't want me telling them they've got to give more. The need to give is not a need anyone feels.*

But giving does connect with two deep human needs. I try to emphasize these needs when speaking about money.

1. *People need to have something of value to sacrifice for.* Somewhere I must find a cause greater than myself, that is worthy of my life, if I am going to count for something. And one way to express commitment to that cause is to give. When you give your money, you really have given yourself.

I think that when Jesus comes to church on Sunday morning, he still sits "over against the treasury" to see what we put into the offering. As a measure of our commitment, our pocketbook beats our hymnbook. If I can read a person's checkbook for a couple of years, I know what he or she thinks is important.

We desperately need to be committed. Otherwise, we have this awful sense of anomie; we sense our lives don't count. Bob Richards, the pole vaulter, used to ask Olympic athletes, "How do you handle the pain?" They never said, "What pain?" They explained that part of the thrill of victory is that it was gut wrenching to achieve.

Part of the thrill of our lives comes when we find a cause worth sacrificing for and then give to the hilt for it.

2. *People need a way to express thanks.* When someone helps us, we want to say thanks, to tell the person how much we appreciated the help. Giving is a tangible, effective way to thank a God of grace and generosity. "As God has prospered you, give," Paul says. The question is not, "How much do I give to stay in the club?" or "What are the dues?" but "How can I say thanks?" Giving is a perfectly appropriate means of thanking God.

When I preach on money with these two needs in mind, it frees me. No longer am I laying on people an unwanted burden. Instead, I am offering people a thirst-quenching opportunity to involve themselves in something that outlasts them, and to express their gratitude to God.

If I can give someone a new mind-set about money, I have built a new person. As a preacher, that's my goal: to implant a new mind-set about how our money relates us to God. There are times when I say, "This is the cause, and this is what we need," but that's the short-term goal. My true goal, the long-range goal, is to change people's mind-set about money, and that's what good preaching will do.

The first major marital argument for most couples, for example, is about money. That was true for Bonnie and me. For my parents, in the New York ghetto, money was security, so they saved it. Bonnie's middle-class parents thought the purpose of money was to use it. After we got married, Bonnie wanted to buy a set of dishes for thirty dollars, a great deal of money in those days. The thought of putting out that kind of money for a set of dishes drove me wacky. And so our first major conflict erupted over buying dishes.

The conflict came from differing mind-sets—not principles our parents had sat down and taught us, but feelings and values we had picked up intuitively.

Many conflicts in the Christian life come because people approach money with a mind-set different from God's. My goal as a preacher is to bring their thinking in line with his.

Knowing this takes the pressure off both me and my listeners. I realize such a change is going to take a long time, and I need to work on it purposefully, not frantically. Without immediate pressure, though, remarkable change does occur. With defenses down, a person alters his or her view over time. Conversion seems sudden, but it's usually the result of a process.

When I taught a businessmen's Bible study in Dallas, a CEO of a computer company attended. Others in the group knew he wasn't a Christian. One day I invited the man to lunch and I asked him, "Wally, are you a Christian?"

"Yes I am."

I thought he may have confused *Christian* with *gentleman*. So I asked him, "When did it happen?"

He replied, "I don't know."

So I said, "Tell me why you call yourself a Christian then."

"When I came to your class, I wasn't a Christian," Wally told me. "One day as I was shaving, I looked in the mirror and thought to myself, *You know, if I stood before God today and he said, 'Why should I let you into heaven?' I would say, 'I'm betting my life on Jesus Christ.'* I wouldn't have said that several weeks ago," he said, "but I know that's what I would say to God now. Someplace in the last month or two, I crossed the line."

Similarly, when teaching on money, I need to teach for the distance rather than the dash, knowing that over time people can change their attitudes and their giving dramatically.

Emphasize Attitude, Not Amount

A third principle I follow is to de-emphasize the amount—even the percentage—that someone gives. Instead, I try to emphasize the element that from a biblical perspective is more critical: The giver's attitude and level of sacrifice.

The gold-medal giver in the New Testament turns out to be a woman who contributed less than a nickel. And on the day she was singled out, wealthy contributors cast generous, lavish gifts into the temple treasury. But this woman slipped in just a couple of coins, and Jesus awarded her the trophy for giving. According to rabbinic law, a giver could not give just one mite; the smallest gift permitted was two mites. On that day, for her, giving to God was more important than a crust of bread, a bit of honey, or a sip of milk. Giving to God was more important than her necessary food. That was worship. Jesus jumped to his feet when he saw her contribution. He shouted to his disciples, "Mark her out. She's someone special."

I believe God honors many poor people who don't give a tenth, because what they do give is a sacrificial amount in relationship to what they earn. Similarly, for many wealthy people, giving a tenth is a way of robbing God. Their tithe becomes a tip.

I'm impressed by the formula of John Wesley, who, when he made thirty pounds, lived on twenty-eight pounds and gave away two. Then he made sixty pounds, but he knew he could live on twenty-eight pounds, so he gave away thirty-two. The next year his income rose to ninety pounds, but still he lived on twenty-eight pounds and gave away the rest.

As we preach, therefore, the key is not to focus on amounts or percentages, but the attitude and commitment the giver displays.

Teach "Investment" Principles

Fourth, I believe we have a responsibility to teach people how to invest their money in God's kingdom. People need sound investment advice, which the Bible provides. Here are some of the strategies I teach.

• *First, cover your obligations.* If you ask, "According to the New Testament, what am I obligated to give to?" the answer would include four areas, concentric circles:

1. To provide food and shelter for your family. To not support them is to be worse than a heretic.
2. To support those who teach you the Word of God.
3. To help those who are poor in the church.
4. To do good to all men and women, as much as you have opportunity.

• *Give thoughtfully and with preparation.* We are taught to "lay aside on the first day of the week" what we will give, so it's irresponsible to get to church and think, *Oh! The offering!* grab your wallet, and throw in a five-dollar bill.

People should thoughtfully consider their own church's ministries and consider other Christian ministries. Do the leaders demonstrate integrity? Do they issue a financial statement showing the way the organization has used their money? Is their money producing spiritual dividends? As Christians, when we give to causes beyond our church, we ought not to give simply because an orphan choir has touched our emotions. We should weigh thoughtfully the ministries we support.

• *Invest in sound ministries that will produce dividends.* Paul's Letter to the Philippians is actually a thank-you letter. He wrote the letter to thank the folks at Philippi for their most recent gift. And in this letter, Paul sees money as investment in God's work—"I'm grateful for this gift, because I know it will bring dividends to your account" (4:17). If you tie that passage into the Parable of the Unjust Steward, the focus of which is to be shrewd and make friends for heaven, you find this: One way in which to make friends who will welcome you into heaven is by investing in the ministry of other people.

I believe that when Bonnie and I get to heaven, she and I will be welcomed by people from Kenya—a country we never visited and a culture we don't know anything about. Why? Because for years we have helped to support a productive missionary couple there. We bought into that ministry, and one day we will withdraw our equity.

That's one of the problems of investing in certain ministries that have been scandal ridden: they didn't make it, spiritually speaking. They failed to produce spiritual dividends. If we had invested money in those ministries, we would have suffered like an investor after a stock market crash.

• *Diversify your kingdom portfolio.* The serious investor is going to put some money in bonds, some in money markets, and some in high-risk venture capital. But he or she is going to diversify for maximum effectiveness.

Similarly, I think it's wise for Christians to have a kingdom portfolio. First, we give to our local church; that's a basic obligation because we are ministered to there and want to support those who teach us God's Word. But then, I want to give some money to an individual or group skilled in evangelism.

Then I want to support groups that are impacting our society. As a Christian, I want to be involved in helping where I can't be physically. I personally can't be involved in most worthwhile causes. But I can support a few of them financially as a way of saying, "I'm for you." For example, Bonnie and I have given to groups serving battered women and to ministries working with college students.

I don't want to sound self-serving, but I think it's wise to invest in a seminary as a long-term investment. It takes years for a crop of students to mature, but eventually the students you support today are going to become missionaries, pastors, and teachers, and they're going to touch many people.

Now, I recognize that many pastors teach the "storehouse" concept, that the tithe belongs to the local church. In a way, a good church with a wide and varied missionary program can be like a mutual fund. Because there are many people investing in the fund, the congregation has power to do things one person couldn't do on his own, and it invests money in valid ministries he or she might not know about otherwise. Many people trust the leaders of the church to manage their kingdom investment. But the principle is the same: they should see to it that their leaders oversee an effective and diversified program of giving.

Illustrating Effectively

Let me mention two areas that are particularly thorny for the person who preaches about money: (1) illustrations and (2) applications.

Recently someone said to me, "Haddon, when I contemplate standing up and talking about money, the thought of illustrations scares me to death. If I talk about the rich giver, I lose my people. If I talk about the super-poor in Bangladesh, I lose them. If I talk about me, I can lose them because they say, 'Well, you're a preacher. You should do that.' Where can I get credible, real-life illustrations about giving?"

That's a touchy problem. But the first area I mine for illustrations, the mother lode, is the Bible itself. Of the thirty-eight parables of Jesus, at least a dozen are devoted to money and to our use of material goods. The Gospels speak a tremendous amount on money; approximately one of every eight verses deals with the subject. As I mentioned, the Philippian letter is a thank-you letter for financial support, and it teaches much. From these sources, we can draw not only insights, but effective illustrations.

Second, I share my own experiences with giving. I want people to know I'm not asking them to do anything I'm not willing to do. But I speak of my giving in a broad way, as I did explaining my "kingdom investments." Usually, specific amounts only become stumbling blocks.

Third, I draw from stories of friends or situations from society. But which of these do I select? With every illustration, I ask, "What is the hidden message? What does this really convey?" Here are some of the messages I want an illustration to get across:

- *Generous people are attractive.* God loves a generous giver, someone who enjoys giving. That's not hard to understand, because so do we. Being generous does something for a person's spirit. I want the illustration to ask, in effect, "Which word would you like to have applied to you: *tight-fisted or generous?*"

- *Giving enables wonderful things to happen in the lives of others.* I want illustrations to show how giving pays off in people's lives. That's what we do at missions conferences: missionaries report the impact our giving has had on people. Paul, for example, could tell the Philippians, "Your giving has enabled me to minister. While I've been here, the gospel has reached the Praetorian Guard."

- *Giving brings us benefits, but not necessarily material ones.* The danger in the illustration of a person who gave $10 and got $50 back is that it encourages a motivation of "give in order to get." But we can show the rich, nonmaterial blessings that accrue from giving. For example, because we love our children, we tried to give them a good education. We were willing to sacrifice our home—anything—to give them that, and we didn't expect anything in return. But now there's great delight for Bonnie and me seeing what that education has produced in the lives of our children and in the people they reach.

- *God can enable us to give more than we thought possible.* When I was board chairman at Twin City Bible Church in Urbana, Illinois, the congregation decided to purchase land and build next to the campus of the University of Illinois, because that's where we believed we could have the greatest impact. But that was an expensive decision, and the congregation really had to stretch.

As I moved among the congregation, talking to people about this commitment, I was amazed at how many would say something like, "I'm working for Kimberly-Clark, and I just got a promotion that almost doubled my salary."

I'd say. "Is that an accident? Or is God allowing you to help fulfill his mission for this church?"

The testimony of God's people is often that having determined to give a gift, God enabled them to give it. I think it's legitimate to use illustrations that demonstrate God's provision in enabling people to give.

Applications That Stick

Although it's wisest to preach on money when it's not needed, often money is needed, and usually preachers are the ones assigned to ask for it. How do you present the need? What do you ask for?

Perhaps you'll resonate with a few of the lessons I have learned:

• *Ask, and do it boldly*. It should be obvious that if the church has a need, and I talk to you about it, at some point I have to make a request. And I need to do it boldly. Otherwise, I'm like an evangelist presenting the gospel but not asking people to commit themselves to Christ.

I paid a high tuition to learn this lesson. When I became president of a seminary, the school had a phone system that was like two cans on a string. We desperately needed a new one, so I visited a businessman and told him we needed to raise twenty thousand dollars for the new phone system. We talked for a while about it, and then he asked, "How much would you like me to give?"

I said, "Well, could you give a thousand dollars?"

He pulled out his checkbook, wrote me a check for a thousand dollars, pushed it across the desk, and said, "You insulted me."

I thought, *I've offended him. I shouldn't have asked him for money.*

But he said, "You asked me for a thousand dollars, but you needed twenty thousand. Either you felt that I wasn't able to give much money, in which case you underestimated where I am financially. Or worse, you thought I had the money but wouldn't give you more, in which case you insulted my generosity. What you need to know is that if a person believes in the cause, you never insult him by asking him to do the big thing. If he can't do the big thing, he can come back and tell you what he can give. But you always suffer and you insult the person when you ask for less rather than more."

What I appreciated about him is that he didn't say, "Now, give me back the check and let me write you another." It cost me money to learn the lesson.

• *Focus on the cause you believe in.* When I was the president of a seminary, I used to speak on behalf of the school. I was not at all embarrassed to ask people to give. I saw it as a tremendous opportunity for people, because I believe in the cause.

Frankly, I'd have a difficult time raising money for myself. But is there a more important cause than the church of Jesus Christ? As preachers, we have committed our lives to it, and it only makes sense to ask others to join us in supporting it.

• *Lead the way.* Whenever I preach about giving, I had better be giving with liberality. How else can I ask others to give? I don't believe you can ask for a significant contribution unless you are giving with generosity yourself.

• *Emphasize that this is a joint effort.* Sometimes a congregation looks at the missionary program as something the missionary committee put together, or the building program as something the elders put together. That's why it is so important that when a church decides its giving, a wide group of people in the church has a voice in it. Then you can honestly say, "We have committed ourselves to this, and now we need to give to support our commitment. "

• *Give non-Christians and visitors the freedom not to give.* While a church budget or project is for the whole church family, it is for the family only. I believe it is critical for church leaders to say, "If you're still on the way to faith, please feel free to pass the offering plate by. The offering, like Communion, is for those who have committed themselves to Jesus Christ. For you, God has a gift: eternal life. We do not want you to think that God is soliciting funds from you. You honor us by being here."

I have found, oddly enough, that when you say that, and people know you mean it, Christians give with greater generosity, and non-Christians are impressed with the free gift God offers them.

Money = Commitment

Why must preachers continue to bring up the subject of money? Why do we teach our people to give, when we know it can be misunderstood?

Because when we discuss money, we're talking about commitment, and commitment is our domain. A commitment is only cheap talk unless a person puts her money behind it. We want people to be serious about Jesus Christ. And we know that if they are serious about Jesus Christ, they will show it in their giving.

Questions to Consider

1. What are the temptations to avoid in preaching about giving?
2. What are the needs of listeners of which preachers need to be aware when preparing to preach about money?
3. What are the principles Robinson follows when preaching on money and giving?
4. What role do illustrations play in sermons on giving?
5. What are the challenges you face when preaching on money—personally and congregationally?

Bookshelf

Carter, William G., ed. *Speaking of Stewardship: Model Sermons on Money and Possessions.* Louisville: Geneva, 1998.

Hoge, Dean, Patrick McNamara, and Charles Zech. *Plain Talk About Churches and Money.* Bethesda, MD: Alban Institute, 1997.

Horton, Michael, ed. *The Agony of Deceit.* Chicago: Moody, 1990.

Ronsvalle, John L., and Sylvia Ronsvalle. *Behind the Stained Glass Windows: Money Dynamics in the Church.* Grand Rapids: Baker, 1996.

Sproul, R. C. *Money Matters.* Wheaton: Tyndale House, 1985.

Testimony of a Checkbook

The late Billy Rose liked to tell about a husband and wife who decided to separate after twenty years of marriage. Anticipating the financial settlement resulting from the divorce, the husband rummaged through a large box of canceled checks. As he did so he came across a faded, yellowed check made out to the hotel where he and his bride had spent their honeymoon, and then another used as an installment on their first car. He fingered a check paid to the hospital at the birth of their daughter and later remembered the feelings he experienced when he wrote out the check for two thousand dollars as the down payment for their first home. Finally, he pushed the box aside and phoned his wife to tell her that too much had been invested in their marriage to throw it away. He asked her to make a fresh start with him.

If you could go through a family's checks, you would read the story of their lives—what they value, how they live, what they save, and how they spend. In fact, our checkbook reveals more about our priorities and the seriousness of our relationship with God than our hymnbook.

That is why Jesus talked so much about money. One-sixth of the gospels, one-third of the parables touch on the subject of stewardship. Jesus was not a fund-raiser. He dealt with money matters because money matters. For some of us it matters too much. Knowing this Jesus warned, "No servant can be the slave of two masters: he will either hate the first and love the second, or treat the first with respect and the second with scorn. You cannot be the slave both of God and money" (Luke 16:13).

Slavery to money is very abstract. My house, my car, my investments do not mean more to me than God. But Jesus did not say that we must serve God more than money. Evaluating our lives to discover what occupies first place is not the proper test. The question is whether we serve money at all.

George Buttrick speaks to this when he observed, "Of all the masters the soul can choose, there are at last only two—God and mammon. All choices, however small, however the alternatives may be disguised are but variants of this choice."

In our society people seldom reveal their salaries publicly, or their net worth, or their giving. We make a determined effort never to discuss our financial affairs in front of friends or relatives or even our children because money is our ultimate reality and to discuss it is to expose what really matters to us. While Americans stamp on their coins, "In God we trust," they often mean "In *this* god we trust."

Either we serve God and use money or we serve money and use God. Yet, few Christians deliberately dedicate their lives to materialism. Wealth is deceitful, Jesus told us, and its bondage subtle. Like the flypaper and the fly, the fly lands on the sticky substance thinking "my flypaper" only to discover that the flypaper says "my fly."

Is Mammon Your God?

Enslavement to riches comes when we build our lives around money and the things it will buy. But how might we determine when we have taken mammon to be our god? Three questions aid in diagnosing the place that money occupies in our experience. First, am I willing to sacrifice things better than money in order to acquire money? For example, the wise man in Proverbs states that "a good name is more desirable than great wealth, the respect of others is better than silver or gold" (Prov. 22:1). If

I sacrifice my reputation, a clear conscience, my wife or children, my spiritual vitality, in a pursuit of money, then money determines my priorities. Only God has a right to do that.

Do I attempt to buy with money what only God can give me? Many things Americans once prayed for they now pay for. Television's "word from the sponsor" assures us that life consists in what we possess. The Kerner Report concerning civil disorders in the last decade indicted television with provoking discontent and stirring the material appetites of ghetto dwellers. Everyone—rich or poor—gets the message. Money can buy anything. Shovel money into the cancer fund, but don't stop dissipating. Juvenile crimes have increased seven times faster than the juvenile population, but don't take young people to church. Send a donation. Get Washington to appropriate money. Money will cure anything. Living in a society where "spend" is the password, we can begin to rely on bank accounts to purchase security, peace of mind, friendships and honor. When I trust money to do for me what only God can do, money has become my god.

Third, does my concern for making money and keeping it overshadow my concern for my, responsibility to God? What worries me? When I shift my mind into neutral where do my thoughts go? While we are to be careful with money, Jesus taught, we are not to be full of care about it. When I am concerned that God be God in my life, I do not have to be worried about life's necessities, for then God assumes responsibility for food and clothing. Speaking about the need for food, Jesus pointed to the birds, "They neither sow nor reap nor gather into barns, and yet your heavenly father feeds them. Are you not of more value than they?" In discussing clothing, Jesus illustrated with a field flower. "Consider the lilies of the field, how they grow. They neither toil nor spin; yet I tell you that Solomon in all his glory was not arrayed like one of these." He does not imply that we can have everything by doing nothing. Birds do search for food. The point is that they don't worry about it (Matt. 6:25–34).

What worries me masters me. God promises not wealth, but enough. Enough for my own needs and enough left over to meet the needs of others. In the Sermon on the Mount, Jesus instructed us to center our lives on God's kingdom, then clothing, food and drink will be ours as well.

In promising to clothe us when we seek God's kingdom, Christ does not promise us rags. Look at how well God clothes the lilies. While hoarding surplus can destroy us, an abundance is not sinful. When wealth comes to us in the will of God, we should be thankful, enjoy it, and not be ashamed of it. In deciding that our money will serve God we recognize that money is not given to us. It is lent to us. It is ours to invest and not ours to keep.

Paul wrote to his young associate, Timothy, words that I apply to many Christians today: "Charge them who are rich in the world's goods that they are not to look down on other people; and warn them not to set their hopes on money, which is untrustworthy, but on God who, out of his riches, gives us all that we need for our happiness. Tell them that they are to do good, and be rich in good works, to be generous and willing to share—this is the way they can save up a good capital sum for the future, if they want to make sure of the only life that is real" (1 Tim. 6:17–19).

uestions to Consider

1. Why did Jesus talk as much as he did about money?
2. What does it mean to be enslaved to money?
3. What three questions does Haddon Robinson suggest we ask ourselves in relation to money?
4. What are your responses to the three questions?
5. What responsibility is it for the Christian to give his or her money to the Lord's work?

Bookshelf

Burkett, Larry. *Giving and Tithing: Includes Serving and Stewardship.* Chicago: Moody, 1998.

Dean, James D. *Breaking Out of Plastic Prison.* Grand Rapids: Revell, 1997.

Foster, Richard J. *The Challenge of the Disciplined Life: Christian Reflections on Money, Sex, and Power.* San Francisco: Harper & Row, 1989.

Hoge, Dean. *Money Matters: Personal Giving in American Churches.* Louisville: Westminster John Knox, 1996.

Vallet, Ronald W. *Stepping Stones of the Steward.* Grand Rapids: Eerdmans, 1989.

Afterword

Haddon W. Robinson's influence upon late twentieth-century preaching has been profound. The chapters in this book represent his thinking on what it means to preach to listeners in this time. His central idea—Big Idea—approach to preaching is more than a methodology, it is a way of thinking about how to preach.

As one of the top twelve preachers of the English-speaking world, Robinson is not only an able practitioner but a competent thinker. His understanding of the rhetorical components in communication, coupled with exegetical insight and listener awareness, enable him to preach what he practices. The collection of chapters in this book demonstrate his breadth of understanding.

Throughout this book Robinson shows the thoughtful reader that preaching is not simply telling people what the Bible says. Preaching involves a life that is God-centered. Preaching includes keen insight into the meaning and application of the text that is clearly communicated. And preaching demonstrates an understanding and appreciation of one's listeners.

All of the chapters in this book come from the conviction that preaching matters, that it is used by God to change lives, to make a difference. As a young boy Robinson wondered what the difference was between the preacher who preached for an hour but it seemed like twenty minutes, and the preacher who preached for twenty minutes and it seemed like an hour.

Throughout his life Haddon Robinson has attempted to answer that question. He has tried to discover the difference.

Through his study and experience Robinson has looked at the question from numerous angles. The chapters in this book make a composite answer to his question. In reading the book preachers are able to discover the answer and make the difference in their own preaching.

That is what Haddon Robinson did in his preaching—he discovered the difference. And that is what this book is intended to do—to help other preachers make the difference.

Notes

Foreword

1. *Cf.* Keith Willhite and Scott M. Gibson, eds., *The Big Idea of Biblical Preaching: Connecting the Bible to People* (Grand Rapids: Baker, 1998).

2. Haddon W. Robinson, *Biblical Preaching: The Development and Delivery of Expository Messages* (Grand Rapids: Baker, 1980), pp. 31–48.

3. James L. Golden and Edward P. J. Corbett, eds., *The Rhetoric of Blair, Campbell and Whately* (New York: Holt, Rinehart and Winston, 1968), p. 298.

Chapter 5

1. Kyle Haselden, *The Urgency of Preaching* (New York: Harper & Row, 1963) 89.

2. R. A. Montgomery, *Expository Preaching* (New York: Revell, 1939) 42.

3. P. T. Forsyth, *Positive Preaching and the Modern Mind* (London and New York: Independent, 1907) 11.

4. F. B. Meyer, *Expository Preaching Plans and Methods* (1910; Grand Rapids: Zondervan, 1954) 58.

Chapter 6

1. Hauch Friedrich, *Theological Dictionary of the New Testament* (Grand Rapids: Eerdmans, 1965) 3:687–88.

2. Examples used to demonstrate the points come from specific sermons preached by people whose position on inspiration would qualify them to join I.C.B.I. My purpose is not to criticize such individuals or to point out their inconsistencies—all of us have nasty homiletical skeletons hanging in our basement—but to illustrate my point. Therefore, I have refrained from giving footnotes for this illustration.

3. R. W. Dale, *Nine Lectures on Preaching* (New York: George H. Doran, 1878), 125.

4. Nathaniel J. Burton, *Yale Lectures on Preaching and Other Writings* (New York: Charles Webster & Company, 1888), 340–41.

5. Donald Miller, *The Way to Biblical Preaching* (Nashville: Abingdon, 1957), 99.

6. Dwight Stevenson, *In The Biblical Preacher's Workshop* (Nashville: Abingdon, 1967), 55.

7. Lloyd Perry, *Manual for Biblical Preaching* (Grand Rapids: Baker, 1965), 107.

8. Heinrich Miller, *Dictionary of New Testament Theology* (Grand Rapids: Zondervan, 1971), 3:906.

9. Sidney Greidanus, *Sola Scriptura* (Toronto: Wedge Publishing Foundation, 1970), 70.

10. Greidanus, 221–22.

11. Greidanus, 225–26.

12. Quoted in *The Way to Biblical Preaching*, 148.

13. Peter Marshall, *John Doe, Disciple* (New York: McGraw-Hill, 1963), 124.

Scott M. Gibson is Assistant Dean and Associate Professor of Ministry at Gordon-Conwell Theological Seminary, South Hamilton, MA, where he teaches homiletics. He earned the Master of Divinity (M.Div.) degree from Gordon-Conwell, the Master of Theology (Th.M.) degree in homiletics from Princeton Theological Seminary, the Master of Theology (M.Th.) degree in Church History from the University of Tornoto, and the Doctor of Philosophy (D. Phil.) degree in church history from the University of Oxford.